FOUR YEARS
WITH
GENERAL LEE

by

WALTER H. TAYLOR

Adjutant-General, Army of Northern Virginia

with a new introduction, index, and notes by

JAMES I. ROBERTSON, JR.

INDIANA UNIVERSITY PRESS
BLOOMINGTON & INDIANAPOLIS

TO THE
EIGHT THOUSAND VETERANS
(THE SURVIVING HEROES OF THE ARMY OF NORTHERN VIRGINIA)
WHO, IN LINE OF BATTLE,
ON THE 9TH DAY OF APRIL, 1865,
WERE REPORTED PRESENT FOR DUTY,
THE FOLLOWING PAGES ARE RESPECTFULLY DEDICATED
BY
THE AUTHOR.

"THOSE who undertake to write histories do not, I perceive, take that trouble on one and the same account, but for many reasons, and those such as are very different one from another. For some of them apply themselves to this part of learning to show their great skill in composition, and that they may therein acquire a reputation for speaking finely. Others of them there are who write histories in order to gratify those that happen to be concerned in them; and on that account have spared no pains, but rather gone beyond their own abilities in the performance. But others there are who, of necessity and by force, are driven to write history, because they were concerned in the facts, and so cannot excuse themselves for committing them to writing, for the advantage of posterity. Nay, there are not a few who are induced to draw their historical facts out of darkness into light, and to produce them for the benefit of the public, on account of the great importance of the facts themselves with which they have been concerned. Now, of these several reasons for writing history, I must profess the last two reasons were my own reasons also." —JOSEPHUS.

Copyright © 1996 by Indiana University Press
Library of Congress Cataloging-in-Publication Data

Taylor, Walter Herron, 1838–1916.
    Four years with General Lee / by Walter H. Taylor ; with a new introduction, index, and notes by James I. Robinson, Jr.
        p.   cm.
    Originally published : Bloomington: Indiana University Press, 1962.
    Includes bibliographical references (p.   ) and index.
    ISBN 0-253-33071-8 (cloth). — ISBN 0-253-21074-7 (pbk.)
    1. United States—History—Civil War, 1861–1865—Campaigns.
2. Lee, Robert E. (Robert Edward), 1807–1870—Friends and associates. 3. Taylor, Walter Herron, 1838–1916. 4. United States—History—Civil War, 1861–1865—Personal narratives, Confederate.
I. Robertson, James I.   II. Title.
E470.2.T25   1996
973.7'82—dc20   95-43897

1 2 3 4 5   01 00 99 98 97 96

INTRODUCTION

Staff officers were among the most underrated but most important components of any Civil War army. They relieved commanding officers of a large amount of minutiae; at the same time, they were a direct link between the general and his subalterns when the former was too occupied for personal meetings. Members of a staff strengthened the necessary chain of command between the ranks and headquarters.

America was late in recognizing the advantages of staff work. Not until 1813 did the Congress create a General Staff at the War Department in Washington. Its basic if not sole purpose was to attend to the housekeeping functions of armies. Staffs in the field were assumed to exist for the same limited reason.

The Civil War was the first of the modern wars: the first all-out struggle in which everything the nation has and does must be brought to bear in the quest for victory. Army generals were not prepared for all that such a conflict entailed. The few commanders appointed to army command in the spring of 1861 had no group of experts or devoted aides who could assist in planning strategic goals, in solving logistical needs, and in attending to those little things that promote smooth and effective administration. Armies in the early stages of the Civil War, one authority has stated, "operated like a team of balky horses."

Increasing attention was therefore given to staffs. The higher ranking the general, the more important became the members of his "inner family." The Southern Confederacy's premier soldier, Gen. Robert E. Lee, commanded as many as 70,000 men in the Army of Northern Virginia. Yet of this host of soldiers who surrounded the incomparable Lee during the war, none enjoyed a closer relationship with the commander than Walter Herron Taylor.

In 1861, this young Virginian became lieutenant and aide de camp to Lee. Four years later, Taylor was lieutenant colonel and assistant adjutant general (the equivalent of chief of staff). Many observers acknowledged that Taylor more than anyone "made himself indispensable to Lee's headquarters." The "extremely efficient" aide "was first to last the closest" of all staff officers to Lee.

What made Taylor's role even more substantial—and what subjects Lee to a measure of criticism—was the small staff that the general drew around him. Lee unselfishly kept his staff to a minimum because he felt that qualified officers were needed more in the ranks. When the stately Virginian assumed command of the South's principal army on June 1, 1862, his staff consisted of an assistant adjutant general, a military secretary, five aides, five clerks, and a handful of couriers. That was insufficient for the huge host Lee put together for a counteroffensive against Union forces threatening Richmond.

The situation improved but little during the three years that Lee commanded in Virginia. Only seven men could be said to have held prominent positions on his staff; only three of them— Charles Marshall, kinsman of the famous chief justice; Charles S. Venable, a mathematics professor; and Walter H. Taylor—attained any distinction. Taylor was the senior of the three in everything but age. Indeed, the general he served so devotedly was almost old enough to be his grandfather.

Taylor was born June 13, 1838, in Norfolk, Virginia. His parents were well-connected and prominent in Tidewater society. The son attended Norfolk Academy and displayed a superior talent for learning. In 1854 Taylor entered the Virginia Military Institute, which had been founded in Lexington only fifteen years earlier. The youth excelled in his first year at the institute. However, the death of his father in a yellow fever epidemic cut short Taylor's hopes for a college education.

He had no choice but to return home to help care for his widowed mother and nine siblings. For the remainder of the 1850s, Taylor worked as a banker and as an auditor for the Norfolk and

Petersburg Railroad. War clouds soon gathered on the horizon. Like hundreds of other young Virginians, Taylor joined a local militia company being formed to defend the Old Dominion's honor. Civil war came, Virginia left the Union, and Taylor entered service as a lieutenant of Company G, 6th Virginia Infantry Regiment.

An infantry career was not to be his lot. One of Gov. John Letcher's chief advisors was Commander Richard L. Page, formerly of the U.S. Navy, an uncle by marriage to Taylor, and a cousin of Robert E. Lee. Another gubernatorial aide was VMI superintendent Francis H. Smith, who remembered Taylor fondly. Thus, on May 2, 1861, the handsome Taylor—still shy of his twenty-third birthday—received orders to report for duty in Richmond to the soldier who was in command of all of Virginia's military forces.

Robert Lee was then one of the most respected of American soldiers. He had spent more than thirty years as army engineer, respected member of Gen. Winfield Scott's staff in Mexico, superintendent of West Point, and colonel of a cavalry regiment. Taylor was awestruck when he first met Lee. "He was then at the zenith of his physical beauty," Taylor declared. "Admirably proportioned, of graceful and dignified carriage, with strikingly handsome features, bright and penetrating eyes, his iron-gray hair closely cut, his face cleanly shaved except a mustache, he appeared every inch a soldier and a man born to command."

Such was the general whom Taylor served for four arduous years. The aide began his staff duty as a first lieutenant, received promotion to captain in December 1861, moved up to major in March 1863, and in December of that year attained his final rank of lieutenant colonel. Taylor was ideally suited for staff work. Hard-working and conscientious, he had above-average intelligence and a finely honed sense of organization. Add to all of that a photographic memory for faces, names, and figures, and it is small wonder that he was the most reliable of Lee's aides.

His wartime duties were many and constant. Taylor wrote the great bulk of Lee's dispatches in a clear, swift script that became as recognizable as his general's signature. He delivered messages from the commanding general to corps and division leaders. It was Taylor who greeted everyone who came to see Lee, and it was usually Taylor who decided whether the petitioner got an audience with the general. The assistant adjutant general attended to a host of details, many of them on his own initiative and without the knowledge of the "Old Man" (as members of the staff affectionately called Lee).

Taylor also had the responsibility of submitting all monthly returns of the Army of Northern Virginia. Hence, and more than any man in the Confederate armies, Walter Taylor knew the effective strength of Lee's force at any given time. Those valuable statistics, along with Taylor's personal reminiscences plus extracts from a few of his wartime letters, are what impart such high value to his first memoir, *Four Years with General Lee.*

Despite the authority he wielded, Taylor was extremely popular with the rank and file in the Confederate forces. Youthful enthusiasm was part of the answer. On at least two occasions, the desire to participate in battle overcame his duties at headquarters. Taylor's gallantry (albeit unauthorized) at both Spotsylvania and Petersburg brought both commendation and lasting esteem.

His love affair with "Bettie" Saunders also underscored Taylor's human qualities. He was barely twelve years old when he fell in love with this daughter of a naval commodore. For the next fifteen years, the two waged an up-and-down courtship. On April 2, 1865, as the Confederacy was disintegrating and the fall of Richmond was imminent, Lee gave Taylor permission to leave the army for a few hours in order to get married.

The wedding of Lee's adjutant and Miss Saunders occurred in St. Paul's Episcopal Church in the capital. "Tears and sobs were the only music," the bride wrote; and when the rector bestowed the final blessing upon the couple, "he too wept."

Taylor dashed back to rejoin Lee's army as it stumbled westward in retreat. Union forces surrounded what was left of "Lee's Miserables" at Appomattox Court House. When the Southern commander had no choice but to meet with Gen. U.S. Grant and discuss terms of surrender, for once Taylor could not bring himself to stand by the side of his chieftain. The twenty-six-year-old colonel found it impossible, he later admitted, to "endure the thought of seeing that heroic soul bowed in agony by the last blow of fate."

Hence, and contrary to popular belief, the lone Confederate aide depicted with Lee in paintings of the surrender scene in Wilmer McLean's parlor is not Taylor but Lt. Col. Charles Marshall, another member of Lee's staff. Taylor was waiting for Lee when the downcast commander returned to his beaten army.

Taylor then had the painful duty of signing the paroles for all the members of the staff except himself. His parole was the only one signed personally by Lee. One final act remained as a benediction to the war. A few days after the surrender, the adjutant stood proudly on Lee's left when noted photographer Matthew Brady took a series of pictures of Lee on the back porch of the Lee family's temporary quarters in Richmond.

The postwar years for Taylor were cheerful and prosperous. He and his wife had eight children, all of whom reached maturity. Taylor founded a hardware business in Norfolk. In 1877 he began a thirty-nine-year tenure as president of the Marine Bank. His outside interests were many; his labors, indefatigable. Taylor was much involved with Episcopal Church affairs, highway construction in the Norfolk area, building and loan associations, and insurance companies. He served a term in the state senate and two terms on the Board of Visitors of the Virginia Military Institute.

Amid all of his many civic and religious endeavors, Taylor also found time to achieve high standing as a writer. A Richmond friend noted: "It was natural that Colonel Taylor, in reality but a boy, should have seen things that others overlooked and that he should in love for his great commander have written of those incidents in volumes that will remain among the classics of Southern history."

Because of his unmatched closeness to Lee, and possessed as he was with instant recall, Taylor was for a half-century after Appomattox "an unofficial court of last resort" where controversies relative to the Army of Northern Virginia were con-

cerned. The Norfolk native had a keen sense of history and recognized its value. He was the first Southerner who asked for,
and received, permission to study captured Confederate records
taken to Washington. Taylor incorporated some of his own
knowledge into that information (which predated the appearance of the first volumes of the mammoth *Official Records of the
Union and Confederate Armies*), and in 1877 he published *Four
Years with General Lee.*

The book was so highly regarded from the outset that it was a
collector's item by the turn of the century. Bowing to countless
requests, Col. Taylor revised his reminiscences, added much new
material from the *Official Records*, and in 1906 brought forth a second memoir, *General Lee, 1861-1865.* The recent publication in
book form of 110 of Taylor's wartime letters not only enhances the
picture of the young chief of staff; it also enriches Taylor's first
published work, which was written soon after the echoes of civil
war died away. The freshness of *Four Years with General Lee*, as well
as the fact that its author was so intimate with the South's greatest
soldier, gives the book a never-ending importance among the vast
literature of that period.

A long and full life came to an end on March 1, 1916, when
Taylor died at the age of seventy-seven. By order of the Virginia
General Assembly, all state flags went to half-mast. Burial was in
Norfolk's Elmwood Cemetery.

One of Virginia's largest newspapers eulogized the former adjutant with these sentiments: "Colonel Taylor was not the type to
vaunt himself. He never boasted of his association with Lee or,
indeed, told in print half he knew of the difficulties under which
the great commander labored. He was modest and unassuming,
yet never hesitated, when called upon, to sustain the record of his
captain against the venom of irreconcilable enemies."

Walter Taylor's Civil War experiences were unique. The young-
est but most valued member of Lee's staff, he was diligent and
dedicated, industrious and intrepid. This book reflects his useful-

ness to the Confederacy's major army. It also explains why and how this individual had the high privilege of signing so many dispatches with lines that have been famous ever since:

> By command of General R. E. Lee,
> W. H. Taylor
> Assistant Adjutant General

JAMES I. ROBERTSON, JR.

VIRGINIA TECH
SUMMER, 1995

left to right: General Lee's son, Custis, General Robert E.
Lee, and Walter H. Taylor

PREFACE.

It was my peculiar privilege to occupy the position of a confidential staff-officer with General Lee during the entire period of the War for Southern Independence. From the time he assumed the duties of the position of general-in-chief of the Army of Virginia; through the campaign in the western portion of the State; during the time of his command in the Department of South Carolina, Georgia, and Florida; while he was charged with the control of the military operations of all the armies of the South, at Richmond; and in all his campaigns, when in command of the Army of Northern Virginia—I had the honor to be at his side. Of necessity, therefore, some facts concerning him and the army movements which he directed are known to me, which are not of public record; and perhaps some value will attach to my statements in regard to those matters of fact which came under my immediate observation, and the recollection of which is still fresh in my memory. I propose to speak of these briefly and with entire candor. The manner of presenting these memoirs will necessarily be very imperfect. It accords neither with my tastes nor the consciousness of my unfitness for me to attempt a work of this character; and, moreover, the duties of my daily life are such as do not permit any continuous or steady devotion to such an under-taking.

But the conviction that it is the duty of every one, in possession of material information relative to the late sectional conflict, to do what he can to insure a true understanding of that struggle, silences those personal scruples which would deter me, and impels me to give to the public the following pages. It will be at once seen that it is not my purpose to attempt a review of the military career of General Lee, nor a critical history of the army which he commanded in the field; this will devolve upon the future historian; mine is the more humble task of giving a summary of the more prominent events in the career of the great Confederate leader, together with a comparative statement of the strength of the Confederate and Federal armies that were engaged in the operations in Virginia. Having for a long time supervised the preparation of the official returns of the Army of Northern Virginia, and having been permitted to make a recent examination of a number of those returns, now on file in the archive-office of the War Department at Washington, I am enabled to speak with confidence of the numerical strength of the Confederate forces; my information concerning that of the Federal forces is derived from official documents emanating from the officers and authorities of the United States Government.

W. H. T.

CONTENTS.

CHAPTER I.

CHAPTER II.

CHAPTER III.

CHAPTER IV.

CHAPTER V.

CHAPTER VI.

FOUR YEARS WITH GENERAL LEE.

CHAPTER I.

Organization of the Army of Virginia.—General R. E. Lee assigned to the Command of the State Troops.—Transfer to the Southern Confederacy.

ON the 2d day of May, 1861, in obedience to telegraphic orders from Governor Letcher, I repaired to Richmond, and was at once assigned to duty at the headquarters of the Army of Virginia. General Lee had been assigned to the chief command, and Colonel Robert S. Garnett had been announced as the adjutant-general of the active State troops. The utmost activity prevailed, and the general-in-chief and his indefatigable and most efficient adjutant-general devoted their entire time and energies to the very difficult task of organizing, arming, equipping, and putting into the field the volunteers, with and without partial organization, who responded with so much alacrity to the call of the State authorities. The first matter of importance was the discussion and decision of the question as to the period of service for which the troops should be received and mustered in. While the politicians, and indeed the vast majority of the people, anticipated but a very short and decisive struggle, General Lee took a different view, and stands alone, of all of those then known to me whose opinions were entitled to consideration, as having expressed his most serious apprehensions of a prolonged and bloody war: he, in an especial degree,

seemed to appreciate the magnitude of the impending contest, and to realize the inevitable suffering, sacrifice, and woe,
which would attend a determined and bitter conflict between
the two sections of the United States, each animated by a
traditional devotion to cherished institutions; each entitled
by inheritance to those characteristic traits of the Anglo-
Saxon race, the possession of which precludes the idea of a
passive resistance or a mild aggression, when liberty and
honor are involved; each falsely estimating the powers and
temper of its adversary, and each confident of success.

At this period there was a considerable display of bom-
bastic rhetoric; the purifying process had not yet begun,
which ultimately proved the metal of men : would-be and
accustomed leaders, not yet stripped of their pretensions,
misled the people; some without judgment discoursed flip-
pantly about the sixty or ninety days' war that we were to
have, demanding only so much time to overcome the entire
Yankee nation.   Many who entertained views equally absurd
were to be found in the North.   Doubtless these patriots of
both sections were content to retire from service at the ex-
piration of their short terms, convinced that, if the war was
not ended, it should have been, and would have been, had
they had the direction of affairs.   No wonder, then, that when
the troops were to be mustered into service there was a decided sentiment in favor of a *twelve months'* enlistment.   Had
General Lee's wishes prevailed, they would have been mustered in *for the war.*   It is not known how far he endeavored
to have his views adopted, beyond the expression of opinion
repeatedly made to those who consulted him in his office, in
my hearing, in favor of the war enlistment.   He contended
that, if the conflict should terminate in twelve months, or
less, the troops would be at once disbanded and no harm
would result; but, if it should be prolonged beyond that
period, then there would be a more urgent need for the
troops than in the beginning; and the Government would
have to deal with the very serious question of the disintegra-

tion and disorganization of the army, and the substitution of recruits for veterans, in the very face of the enemy.   The civil authorities, however, were loath to believe that there could possibly be any need of troops beyond the period of twelve months, and accordingly the men were enlisted for that time.   The same course had been pursued in the other States in their volunteer organizations; and thus was the first step taken toward creating the necessity for the law of *conscription* which was subsequently enacted by the Confederate Congress.

Under the direction of General Lee, with the aid of the extraordinary administrative ability of Colonel Garnett, the cordial support of the Governor, and the hearty coöperation of a most efficient corps of State officials, the Virginia volunteers were in a wonderfully short time organized, armed, equipped, and sent to the front: so that when the Confederate authorities assumed control of affairs after the State had formally joined the Confederacy, Governor Letcher was enabled to turn over to them the " Army of Virginia," volunteers and provisional, thoroughly organized and ready for work, and around which, as a nucleus, was collected what afterward became the historic " Army of Northern Virginia." The capital of the Confederacy was removed from Montgomery to Richmond, and the various departments of the Government immediately transferred to the latter city ; the War Department carried on the process of organization and preparation ; the functions of General Lee as general-in-chief of the Army of Virginia terminated, and he was created one of the five generals provided for by a law of Congress, in the Army of the Confederate States.   Brigadier-General G. T. Beauregard [1] and General J. E. Johnston, already in the field, were assigned to the command of the troops in Virginia—the former having the " Army of the Potomac " (Confederate States Army) and the latter the forces

[1] General Beauregard was promoted to be General immediately after the first battle of Manassas.

then collected in the lower Valley of Virginia; these two armies were subsequently united and won the first battle of* Manassas under General J. E. Johnston. General A. S. Johnston had been assigned to the command of the troops raised in the West and Southwest, and which were concentrating in Kentucky and Tennessee.

CHAPTER II.

AFTER the transfer of the Virginia forces to the Confederate States, and there being then no suitable command in the field to which General Lee could be assigned, he was retained in Richmond by the President to give the benefit of his counsel and advice in all the important measures involved in the stupendous undertaking of suddenly transforming an agricultural people into a nation of soldiers, prepared for immediate war. During the month of July, 1861, in obedience to the orders of Mr. Davis, he made a personal examination of the troops and defenses around Norfolk, and also paid a visit of inspection to the Army of the Potomac (C. S. A.). At this period the President became very anxious concerning the condition of affairs in the western portion of Virginia. In the northwest the Confederate forces under Brigadier-General Robert S. Garnett (who, when relieved as adjutant-general of the Army of Virginia, had been appointed brigadier-general in the Confederate army, and assigned to the command of the troops in this section) had suffered defeat, and the brave Garnett himself, while endeavoring to rally his troops at Carricksford, had received a mortal wound. Brigadier-General W. W. Loring, had been assigned as his successor in the command of this department, and having collected the scattered remnants of Garnett's little army, together with such reënforcements as the Government had been able to send to his relief, had taken position at Valley Mountain. In the southwest Brigadier-Generals Floyd and Wise were operating under great disadvantages; each having an independent command, and neither being disposed to act a part subordinate to the other. It was impossible, under such circumstances, to secure harmonious action or any united and spirited effort to resist the enemy. There was an evident and imperative need in this quarter for the personal presence of some one who could both restore confidence to the troops and compel the respect and subordination of commanders. General Lee, of all men the most fit for this duty, was also the most available. A battle, however, appeared imminent at this juncture between the two armies facing each other in the neighborhood of Manassas: it was a critical time, and the President suspended the execution of his designs as to Western Virginia until that crisis was passed; but immediately after the first battle of Manassas General Lee was dispatched to the scene of operations in that department to reconcile the differences between Brigadier-Generals Floyd and Wise, and to aid Brigadier-General Loring in the reorganization and recruiting of the shattered forces of Garnett, so that, with the aid of the reönforcements sent, the army there collected might be put in such condition as to prevent any aggressive movement of the enemy, and, if circumstances justified it, to take the offensive. Accompanied by two aides-de-camp—Colonel John A. Washington and myself—he proceeded by rail to Staunton, and thence on horseback to Valley Mountain. Upon his arrival there he established himself near the headquarters of General Loring, with whom he maintained regular and constant communication. He never assumed immediate personal command of the army, although it was understood that Brigadier-General Loring was subject to his orders.

It is useless to attempt to recount all the difficulties this little army encountered in that most impracticable, inhospitable, and dismal country; only those who participated in that campaign can ever properly estimate the disadvantages under which commanders and troops operated. The season was a most unfavorable one: for weeks it rained daily and in torrents; the condition of the roads was frightful; they were barely passable. It was very seriously debated whether the army could be fed where it was, and it was feared that it would have to retire to some point nearer the railroad. Time and time again could be seen double teams of horses struggling with six or eight barrels of flour, and the axle of the wagon scraping and leveling the road-bed; in other words, the wagons were hub-deep in mud, and could only be moved step by step, and then with the greatest difficulty. At the same time, and doubtless as a result of the excessive rains, the troops were sorely afflicted with measles and a malignant type of fever, which prostrated hundreds of each command; and, being entirely destitute of proper food and other supplies indispensable to the successful treatment of disease, it is not to be wondered at that medical skill failed to arrest the terrible scourge.

In the subsequent campaigns of the Army of Northern Virginia the troops were subjected to great privations and to many very severe trials—in hunger often; their nakedness scarcely concealed; strength at times almost exhausted—but never did I experience the same heart-sinking emotions as when contemplating the wan faces and the emaciated forms of those hungry, sickly, shivering men of the army at Valley Mountain! I well recall the fact that a regiment of North Carolina volunteers, under Colonel Lee, that reported with one thousand effective men, was in a very short time reduced to one-third of its original strength, without ever having been under fire. Though not to the same extent, the other commands were all seriously reduced by disease; and it is no exaggeration to say that one-half of the army was ineffective. Moreover, although some of our best and bravest men were from that section, there was great disaffec-

tion among that portion of the people who had not responded to the call of the State for troops.   Spies lurked around
every hill ; our weakness, our embarrassments, and our every
movement, were promptly reported to the enemy.   With
some honorable exceptions, there was an utter absence of
sympathy on the part of the inhabitants who had remained
at home, and, to all intents and purposes, we were in an
enemy's country.   In the language of another who witnessed
this deplorable hostility : " Northwestern Virginia has
brought grief and shame to the State and to the South by
her woful defection ; but by none is that felt more keenly
than by those sons of that section who have left their homes,
and in many instances their wives and little ones, to battle
for the right.   They hear jeers and sneers thrown out, even
at themselves, and endure them with apparent patience, but
with an inward resolve to testify on the battle-field their
fidelity to their country's cause."

How little was this lamentable condition of affairs in that
department then appreciated by the public mind !

From the reputation which General Lee enjoyed, even
at that date, much was expected of him when he took the
field.   The difficulties of his situation were not properly
estimated, and the press and people of Virginia became, at
first, impatient, then indignant, because the Federal army
that had defeated the Confederate forces under Garnett and
Pegram was not immediately assailed by him and driven out
of the State.

To those who realized the situation it was an occasion of
pain and mortification to learn from the journals of the day,
that occasionally reached them, of the general dissatisfaction
that found expression in scathing editorials, abounding in
sneers and abuse, and which was both unjust to those charged
with the conduct of military operations in that impracticable region, and well calculated to dishearten the men under
their command, whose trials were already of no ordinary
character.

No one felt this public judgment so keenly as did General Lee; and yet, on one occasion, when his attention had been directed to a fierce newspaper attack, as unjust in its conclusions as it was untrue in its statements, and he was asked why he silently suffered such unwarranted aspersions, he calmly replied that, while it was very hard to bear, it was perhaps quite natural that such hasty conclusions should be announced, and that it was better not to attempt a justification or defense, but to go steadily on in the discharge of duty to the best of our ability, leaving all else to the calmer judgment of the future and to a kind Providence.

CHAPTER III.

BUT, to return to our narrative, despite the embarrassments heretofore alluded to, the command was finally brought
to a sufficiently efficient condition to induce the general to
take the offensive.   On the 8th of September, and after full
conference with Brigadier-General Loring, the order of attack
was prepared ; it was issued, however, in the name of the
latter, and prescribed a line of operations which I will now
attempt to describe.   In order to a correct understanding of
what is to follow, it is proper to make some remarks upon
the character and prominent features of the immediate locality which was to be the scene of operations, and of the
strength and positions of the two armies.

The advance force of the enemy held the Cheat Mountain
Pass, where the Staunton and Parkersburg turnpike crossed
the centre-top of Cheat Mountain range, about twelve miles
east of Huttonsville.   Just where the road crossed the moun-
tain-top heavy defensive works had been constructed.   Nature assisted in no small degree to render the position impregnable : the descent on both sides was very precipitous,
and the surface of the earth was covered with a most remarkable undergrowth of laurel, so dense and interlocked as
to be almost impenetrable.   The Federals had cleared a considerable space around their intrenched position, constructed

abatis and fosses around their entire work, and, having a garrison of three thousand men,[1] might well have deemed themselves impregnable.

They also held a strongly-fortified position at Elk Water, on the road running from Valley Mountain through Tygart's Valley to Huttonsville, at which latter place it intersected the Staunton and Parkersburg turnpike. The force in Tygart's Valley was estimated to be five thousand strong. The reserve force was stationed at Huttonsville, and here also was their depot for supplies.

The two roads, mentioned as uniting at Huttonsville, were the only practicable routes by which that point could be reached from the east; both, as before explained, were protected by works of formidable aspect and difficult approach. General Reynolds was in command of the troops defending the passes of Cheat Mountain, and had an army estimated at from eight to ten thousand men. General Rosecrans commanded the entire Federal force operating in Western Virginia, embracing that under General Reynolds, and that operating in the Kanawha Valley, under General Cox.

One portion of the Confederate army was encamped at " Camp Bartow," on the Parkersburg pike, near its crossing of the Greenbrier River. The force upon this line was under the immediate command of Brigadier-General H. R. Jackson, and consisted of the following organizations : First Georgia Regiment (Colonel Ramsay), Twelfth Georgia (Colonel Edward Johnson), Twenty-third Virginia (Colonel William B. Taliaferro), Thirty-first Virginia (Colonel Jackson), Thirty-seventh Virginia (Colonel Fulkerson), Forty-fourth Virginia (Colonel Scott), Third Arkansas (Colonel Rust), Hansbrough's and Reger's battalions of Virginia Volunteers, two batteries of artillery, and a few companies of cavalry—in all about twenty-five hundred effective men.

---

[1] A requisition for rations for three thousand men was found upon the person of a staff-officer captured while pursuing the road from Cheat Mountain Pass to Huttonsville.

The other wing of the army, under General Loring, was camped at Valley Mountain, and consisted of a brigade (under General D. S. Donelson) of one North Carolina and two Tennessee regiments; a brigade of Tennessee troops (under General Anderson); a brigade (under Colonel William Gilham) consisting of the Twenty-first and Forty-second Virginia Regiments, and the Irish Battalion (Provisional Army of Virginia); a small command under Colonel Burk; and a battalion of cavalry, under Major W. H. F. Lee.

These commands had been greatly reduced by sickness, and the total effective of this wing of the army did not exceed thirty-five hundred men.

Being without accurate maps of the country, and having no regular engineer-officer available, General Loring had to rely upon his scouts and a few citizens of that country, who acted in a volunteer capacity as guides, for all information as to the roads, and the movements and positions of the enemy. One of these citizen volunteers, a professional surveyor, having been informed that General Lee was particularly anxious to obtain accurate information of the nature and extent of the works of the enemy on the centre-top of Cheat Mountain, undertook the task of reaching such a point on the mountain as would enable him to take a deliberate and careful survey of the fortified position. He was also to ascertain and report if it was practicable to lead a body of infantry to the vicinity of that point, by any route which would prevent the disclosure of the movement.

The only route other than the turnpike by which this point of the range of mountains could be reached was by pursuing a course along and up the precipitous and ragged sides of the mountain, through undergrowth and trees, over rocks and chasms, and with nothing save the compass or the stars to indicate the direction of the summit. The *quasi* engineer-officer made the ascent successfully, and obtained a complete view of the enemy's works. On a second reconnaissance he was accompanied by Colonel A. Rust, of the

Third Arkansas Regiment, who was very enterprising, and appeared to be most anxious to make a personal observation. Together they made the ascent of the mountain, and again complete success crowned their efforts. A full, unobstructed view of the entire line of works occupied by the enemy was had without discovery. On their return they made their report to General Lee, and represented that the works were of such a character as to justify the hope of being carried, if attacked from the direction of the point reached by them, from which they could plainly see all that was going on within; and on which flank the enemy appeared to have be-stowed but little attention. The only difficulty was, to reach this point with a body of troops without attracting the atten-tion of the enemy, so that he might be surprised and the more readily captured. Of the successful accomplishment of this, however, Colonel Rust was sanguine, and enthusiasti-cally asked to be permitted to lead a column in an assault upon this position. General Lee decided to give battle. A column of infantry twelve hundred strong, consisting of the Twenty-third, Thirty-first, and Thirty-seventh Virginia Regi-ments, the Third Arkansas Regiment, and Hansbrough's Virginia battalion, was selected to assail the works of the enemy on Centre-top. Colonels Taliaferro and Fulkerson, who were senior in rank to Colonel Rust, magnanimously waived the question of rank, and acquiesced in placing them-selves at the head of their respective regiments and under Colonel Rust's command.

The order of battle directed General H. R. Jackson to advance, with the balance of his command, by the turnpike, and to threaten the enemy from this direction—this was especially designed to divert attention from Rust's flank-movement.

The third column, under Brigadier-General Anderson, was to advance to the third or west top of Cheat Mountain, secure possession of the turnpike at that point, and be in position both to take the enemy in rear and prevent any escape; as also to resist any effort that might be made to re-enforce Centre-top with any troops that might be in reserve.

The rest of the army was to move down the valley of Tygart's River upon the enemy there stationed; but, as will appear more fully hereafter, the movements of this column were made to depend upon the success which should attend the assault upon the fortified position on Cheat Mountain. The plan of attack was carefully and maturely considered, and was communicated to the commanders in the following order:

[CONFIDENTIAL.]

HEADQUARTERS, VALLEY MOUNTAIN, *September* 8, 1861.

[Special Order No. 28.]

1. General H. R. Jackson, commanding Monterey division, will detach a column of not more than two thousand men under Colonel Rust, to turn the enemy's position at Cheat Mountain Pass at daylight on the 12th instant (Thursday).

During the night preceding the morning of the 12th instant, General Jackson having left a suitable guard for his own position with the rest of his available force, will take post on the eastern ridge of Cheat Mountain, occupy the enemy in front, and coöperate in the assault of his attacking column should circumstances favor. The march of Colonel Rust will be so regulated as to attain his position during the same night, and at the dawn of the appointed day (Thursday, 12th) he will, if possible, surprise the enemy in his trenches and carry them.

2. The "Pass" having been carried, General Jackson, with his whole fighting force, will immediately move forward toward Huttonsville, prepared against an attack from the enemy, taking every precaution against firing upon the portion of the army operating west of Cheat Mountain, and ready to coöperate with it against the enemy in Tygart's Valley. The supply-wagons of the advancing columns will follow, and the reserve will occupy Cheat Mountain.

3. General Anderson's brigade will move down Tygart's Valley, following the west slope of Cheat Mountain range, concealing his movements from the enemy. On reaching Wyman's

(or the vicinity) he will refresh his force unobserved, send forward intelligent officers to make sure of his further course, and during the night of the 11th (Wednesday) proceed to the Staunton turnpike where it intersects the west top of Cheat Mountain, so as to arrive there as soon after daylight on the 12th (Thursday) as possible. He will make dispositions to hold the turnpike, prevent reënforcements reaching Cheat Mountain Pass, cut the telegraph-wire, and be prepared, if necessary, to aid in the assault of the enemy's position on the middle top of Cheat Mountain by General Jackson's division, the result of which he must await. He must particularly keep in mind that the movement of General Jackson is to *surprise* the enemy in their defenses. He must, therefore, not discover his movement, nor advance—before Wednesday night—beyond a point where he can conceal his force. Cheat Mountain Pass being carried, he will turn down the mountain and press upon the left and rear of the enemy in Tygart's Valley, either by the old or new turnpike, or the Becky Run road, according to circumstances.

4. General Donelson's brigade will advance on the right of Tygart's Valley River, seizing the paths and avenues leading from that side to the river, and driving back the enemy that may endeavor to retard the advance of the centre along the turnpike, or turn his right.

5. Such of the artillery as may not be used on the flanks will proceed along the Huttonsville turnpike, supported by Major Munford's battalion, followed by the rest of Colonel Gilham's brigade in reserve.

6. Colonel Burk's brigade will advance on the left of Tygart's Valley River, in supporting distance of the centre, and clear that side of the valley of the forces of the enemy that might obstruct the advance of the artillery.

7. The cavalry under Major Lee will follow, according to the nature of the ground, in rear of the left, Colonel Burk's brigade. It will watch the movements of the enemy in that quarter; give notice of, and prevent, if possible, any attempt to turn the left of the line, and be prepared to strike when opportunity offers.

8. The wagons of each brigade, properly parked and

guarded, under the charge of their respective quartermasters—
who will personally superintend their movements—will pursue
the main turnpike, under the general direction of the chief
quartermaster, in rear of the army and out of cannon-range of
the enemy.

9. Commanders on both lines of operations will particularly see that their corps wear the distinguishing badge, and
that both officers and men take every precaution not to fire on
our own troops. This is essentially necessary, as the forces on
both sides of Cheat Mountain may unite. They will also use
every exertion to prevent noise and straggling from the ranks,
correct quietly any confusion that may occur, and cause their
commands to rapidly execute their movements when in presence
of the enemy.

By order of General W. W. LORING :

CARTER L. STEVENSON,
Assistant Adjutant and Inspector General.

On the same day that General Loring issued the order
of march and attack to his army, General Lee issued the following :

HEADQUARTERS, VALLEY MOUNTAIN, *September* 8, 1861.

[Special Order No. —.]

The forward movement announced to the Army of the Northwest in Special Order No. 28, from its headquarters, of this
date, gives the general commanding the opportunity of exhort-
ing the troops to keep steadily in view the great principles for
which they contend, and to manifest to the world their determination to maintain them. The eyes of the country are upon
you. The safety of your homes, and the lives of all you hold
dear, depend upon your courage and exertions. Let each man
resolve to be victorious, and that the right of self-government,
liberty and peace, shall in him find a defender. The progress
of this army must be forward.

R. E. LEE,
General commanding.

Inasmuch as Rust's column had the most difficult part to perform, and it was impossible to estimate accurately the time which would be consumed in reaching his point of attack, he was started in advance of the other columns, and it was determined and ordered that they should await the signal of his attack, before doing anything more than securing positions from which they could readily and quickly advance to the work to which they had been respectively assigned. All were ordered to take every precaution to prevent their movements from being discovered, as the success of the whole undertaking depended on taking the enemy on Centre-top by surprise. Although the several tops of the mountain were in a direct line, not very distant from each other, it was necessary to make a considerable circuit in riding from one to the other; and as Rust's musketry could be more readily and promptly observed than any other signal, the general attack was made to depend upon it.

The several commands, being in every respect prepared for the anticipated battle, moved forward at the time mentioned, and in the several directions indicated, in the order of march and attack.

All progressed satisfactorily. Anderson reached and occupied the turnpike at its crossing on the third or rear top of Cheat Mountain. So unsuspecting was the enemy, and so silently was Anderson's movement made, that his men captured an engineer-officer of Rosecrans's staff, and others, quietly and confidently pursuing the road toward their rear.

General Jackson had his command well in hand, prepared to engage the enemy in front.

General Donelson's brigade rested the latter portion of the night not far from the camps of his enemy on Tygart's Valley River.

Morning found everything just as the most confident could have hoped, with the exception that the night had been a very rainy, disagreeable one, and the men were consequently quite uncomfortable; this, however, would soon be forgotten in the excitement of battle and the promise of certain victory. All was ready, and Rust's attack was anxiously awaited. General Jackson worried the enemy considerably by attacking his advanced guard on the first top of the mountain, only awaiting the signal from Rust to press forward earnestly with his entire command. Hours passed, and no signal was heard! What could have happened? Enough time had elapsed to enable the troops to reach Centre-top, unless prevented by some unexpected impediment.

Would Rust *never* attack? Alas! he never did!

As was subsequently learned, upon an examination of the works of the enemy made after he had succeeded in reaching his proper position, he was surprised to find them far more formidable than he had supposed. Whether additional strength had been given them since his reconnaissance, or whether he was too easily satisfied and not sufficiently thorough in his observations when he made that reconnaissance, is not known. He decided that the works were too formidable to justify an assault, and no attack was made. Even had he discharged his guns and vigorously engaged the enemy, without attempting to carry the works by storm, it is not unreasonable to believe that the combined efforts of the other columns would have been attended with success.

All, however, depended on the enemy's being surprised, and simultaneously and swiftly attacked. Much precious time had been lost. Donelson's men, uneasy about their arms, fearful that their powder had been dampened by the rain, commenced a spirited fusillade in order to reload and avoid a "flash in the pan." This and Jackson's activity aroused the enemy: hurried preparations to resist attack were made; scouting-parties of cavalry were sent out to scour the surrounding country. One of these detachments came very near capturing General Lee, who, accompanied by his aide and a few horsemen, on his way to join General Donelson, had scarcely emerged from a piece of woods, when quite a troop thundered along the road skirting the woods, too near to be comfortable, but galloping rapidly away on suddenly observing their proximity to Donelson's column of infantry. It was also in a brush between one of these detachments of the enemy and a portion of Major W. H. F. Lee's battalion of cavalry that the pious Christian and gallant gentleman, Colonel John A. Washington, who had been sent with Major Lee to reconnoitre the enemy, was shot dead from an ambuscade.

Detached, discovered, without knowledge of the cause of Rust's silence, the other commands were powerless for good. Occupied with the necessity of providing for their own safety, it only remained to have them recalled to their former positions. The enemy made no advance, and, beyond driving in their outposts, our troops were not seriously engaged.

On the next day Colonel Rust personally reported to General Lee. The only cause assigned by him for his non-action is that heretofore given. Possibly his regimental commanders may have agreed with him in esteeming the works of the enemy too formidable to be attacked; but surely the responsibility attached to him alone.[1]

Some may think that this was a proper matter for investigation by a court of inquiry, or for trial by court-martial. Neither the one nor the other was ever had, and possibly

[1] "By this time most of the command had come up, and a council of war was held as to what we should do, consisting of Colonels Rust, Taliaferro, and Fulkerson, and Lieutenant-Colonels Barton, Jackson, and Hansbrough. It should be here stated that none of the officers were fully apprised of the plan of combined attack, and of the fact that everything depended on the ball being set in motion by our command, except Colonel Rust.

"I shall never forget the appearance of the officers composing this council; Fulkerson looked pale and worn, but intrepid; Taliaferro stern but indifferent. The latter soon broke off the deliberations by saying, 'Well, if we have to fight these people, let's do it at once.' Immediately the rear of the column was deployed around to the right, while we who had led the file remained on the left; and there we stood anxiously awaiting the word to advance to the assault. This word never came."—Extract from letter of Lieutenant-Colonel G. W. Hansbrough.

no public good would have resulted had either been convened.

Having failed to dislodge the enemy from his stronghold, the season having advanced too far to attempt any movement away from our base of supplies, and there being no probability of any serious advance by the enemy, the campaign in the northwest was regarded as ended for the winter.

The following letter from General Lee to Governor Letcher, but recently made public, serves to confirm what has been stated:

VALLEY MOUNTAIN, *September* 17, 1861.

MY DEAR GOVERNOR: I received your very kind note of the 5th instant just as I was about to accompany General Loring's command on an expedition to the enemy's works in front, or I would have before thanked you for the interest you take in my welfare, and your too flattering expressions of my ability. Indeed, you overrate me much, and I feel humbled when I weigh myself by your standard. I am, however, very grateful for your confidence, and I can answer for my sincerity in the earnest endeavor I make to advance the cause I have so much at heart, though conscious of the slow progress I make. I was very sanguine of taking the enemy's works on last Thursday morning. I had considered the subject well. With great effort the troops intended for the surprise had reached their destination, having traversed twenty miles of steep, rugged mountain-paths; and the last day through a terrible storm which lasted all night, and in which they had to stand drenched to the skin in cold rain. Still their spirits were good. When morning broke, I could see the enemy's tents on Valley River at the point on the Huttonsville road, just below me. It was a tempting sight. We waited for the attack on Cheat Mountain, which was to be the signal. Till 10 A. M. the men were cleaning their unserviceable arms. *But the signal did not come.* All chance for a surprise was gone. The provisions of the men had been destroyed the preceding day by the storm. They had had nothing to eat that morning, could not hold out another day, and were obliged to be withdrawn. The party sent to Cheat Mountain to take that in rear had also to be withdrawn. *The attack to come off from the east side failed from the difficulties in the way;* the opportunity was lost, and our plan discovered. It is a grievous disappointment to me, I assure you. But for the rain-storm, I have no doubt it would have succeeded. This, Governor, is for your own eye. Please do not speak of it; we must try again. Our greatest loss is the death of my dear friend Colonel Washington. He and my son were reconnoitring the front of the enemy. They came unawares upon a concealed party who fired upon them within twenty yards, and the colonel fell pierced by three balls. My son's horse received three shots, but he escaped on the colonel's horse. His zeal for the cause to which he had devoted himself carried him, I fear, too far.

We took some seventy prisoners, and killed some twenty-five or thirty of the enemy. Our loss was small besides what I have mentioned. Our greatest difficulty is the roads. It has been raining in these mountains about six weeks. It is impossible to get along. It is that which has paralyzed all our efforts. With sincere thanks for your good wishes,

I am, very truly yours,

R. E. LEE.

His Excellency Governor JOHN LETCHER.

CHAPTER IV.

MEANWHILE the Federal commander had been active in the Kanawha Valley, and, owing to matters of discord between Generals Floyd and Wise, it became imperatively necessary for General Lee to repair to that quarter, in order to restore harmony among our own people, and to resist the further advance of the enemy. Simultaneously General Rosecrans moved with a large portion of his army to reën‑force General Cox; and General Lee ordered General Loring to leave a sufficient force to watch the enemy at Cheat Mountain, and move with the rest of his army to the Kanawha Valley.

General Lee proceeded without delay across the country in that direction.

On the 14th of September General Floyd encamped on Big Sewell Mountain, and ordered General Wise to go into camp a short distance east of him. On the night of the 16th he retreated to Meadow Bluff, directing General Wise to cover the movement and follow with his command to that point. This order General Wise positively refused to obey; and, selecting a favorable position on Little Sewell Mountain, he proceeded to make it good by a line of defensive works.

Such was the condition of affairs as reported to General Lee, who, upon his arrival, found General Floyd with his command at Meadow Bluff, and General Wise some ten or more miles in advance, at Little Sewell, with his legion of seventeen hundred men, now confronted by Rosecrans's entire army.

Without entering into the merits of the controversy between Generals Floyd and Wise, General Lee perceived at a glance that Little Sewell was the most favorable point at which to make a stand ; that being naturally a strong position, and much more easily defended than Meadow Bluff. General Floyd was therefore at once ordered to move forward to Little Sewell. The bitter feeling which had been engendered between the two commanders had imparted itself, in some degree, to the troops, and seriously threatened to impair their efficiency. No little diplomacy was required, therefore, to produce harmony and hearty coöperation, where previously had prevailed discord and contention. It will be readily understood that the partisans of Floyd at first viewed in no pleasant frame of mind the apparent indorsement of Wise's judgment, if not, by a forced construction (to which a prejudiced mind is always liable), the approval of his disobedience and insubordination, implied in General Lee's order that Floyd should forsake his chosen position and return to that persistently held by Wise.

A junction of the commands of Floyd and Wise having been effected, a line of defense was established, and as well fortified as circumstances would admit in that broken country.

The reënforcements from Loring's army soon arrived, and the aggregate strength of the troops under General Lee was, in round numbers, about eight or nine thousand men.

Soon after the arrival of General Lee a messenger came with an order from the President, relieving General Wise of his command, and directing him to repair to Richmond for assignment to another field of duty of equal importance and dignity.

I express no opinion in regard to the matters of difference between Generals Floyd and Wise, and no conclusion prejudicial to the latter should be drawn from the action of the War Department, relieving him of his command. General Lee, so far as is known to me, never undertook to ascertain or decide the merits of the controversy between those officers; but, as the good of the service required that one or the other should be relieved from duty with that army, an order to that effect was issued by direction of the President, and with General Lee's concurrence.

The combined forces of the enemy, under Generals Rosecrans and Cox, were estimated to be from twelve to fifteen thousand strong.[1]

With such an army, elated by its previous encounters with the small force heretofore opposed to it, it was reasonably presumed that the Federal commander would continue on the aggressive. General Lee caused every preparation to be made to give battle. He was but too recently on the field to adopt any other than a defensive policy: he had already demonstrated his unwillingness to recede, by the advance from Meadow Bluff to Little Sewell Mountain. The enemy held a strong position on Big Sewell Mountain, from which, as a base, he had already advanced to engage the troops of General Wise. There was no reasonable cause to doubt that General Rosecrans, who was now in command, would continue this advance, and assail the Confederate position. It was a matter of great surprise, therefore, when, on the morning of the 6th of October, it was discovered that the enemy was no longer in our front; and this surprise was increased when, on pursuing the road over which Rosecrans's army had retreated, it was evident, from the manner in which provisions and accoutrements had been tumbled out or left upon the route, that the flight had been somewhat precipitate and disorderly.

We had now reached the latter days of October: the

---

[1] This was a great exaggeration on the part of the Confederates. General Rosecrans puts his effective strength at this time at but eight thousand five hundred.—"Report on the Conduct of the War," Second Series, vol. iii., p. 10.

lateness of the season and the condition of the roads precluded the idea of earnest aggressive operations, and the campaign in Western Virginia was virtually concluded.

Judged from its results, it must be confessed that this series of operations was a failure. At its conclusion a large portion of the State was in possession of the Federals, including the rich valleys of the Ohio and Kanawha Rivers, and so remained until the close of the war. For this, however, General Lee cannot be reasonably held accountable. Disaster had befallen the Confederate arms, and the worst had been accomplished, before he reached the theatre of operations; the Alleghanies then constituted the dividing line between the hostile forces, and in this network of mountains, sterile and rendered absolutely impracticable by a prolonged season of rain, Nature had provided an insurmountable barrier to operations in the transmontane country.

It was doubtless because of similar embarrassments that the Federal general retired, in the face of inferior numbers, to a point nearer his base of supplies.

During the time that General Lee was in this department (his first service in the field under Confederate auspices), he manifested that complete self-abnegation and dislike for parade and ceremony which later in the war became characteristic of him. Accompanied originally by a staff of but two persons, and, after the death of Colonel Washington, with but one aide-de-camp, with no escort nor body-guard, no couriers nor guides, he made the campaign under altogether unostentatious and really uncomfortable circumstances. One solitary tent constituted his headquarters-camp; this served for the general and his aide; and when visitors were entertained, as actually occurred, the general shared his blankets with his aide, turning over those of the latter to his guest. His dinner-service was of tin—tin plates, tin cups, tin bowls, everything of tin—and consequently indestructible; and to the annoyance and disgust of the subordinates, who sighed for porcelain, could not or would not be lost; indeed, with the help of occasional additions, this tin furniture continued to do service for several campaigns; and it was only in the last year of the war, while the army was around Petersburg, that a set of china was surreptitiously introduced into the baggage of the headquarters of the army. This displaced for a time the chaste and elaborate *plate;* but on resuming "light marching order" at the time of the evacuation of Richmond and Petersburg, the china, which had been borrowed by the staff, was returned; the tins were again produced and did service until the surrender of the army, when they passed into the hands of individuals who now preserve them as mementos of the greatest commander in the great war.

CHAPTER V.

General Lee repairs to Richmond.—He is ordered to the Department of South Carolina, Georgia, and Florida.—His Return thence to Richmond.—He is charged with the Control of the Military Operations of all of the Confederate Armies.—His Duties in that Position.—General Johnston wounded in the Battle of Seven Pines.—General Lee in Command of the Army of Northern Virginia.—The Seven Days' Battles around Richmond.—Strength of the Two Opposing Armies.

SOON after the occurrences in Western Virginia just related, General Lee returned to Richmond and resumed his position and duties as adviser and counselor to the President. On the 6th of November, 1861, he proceeded to South Carolina for the purpose of directing and supervising the construction of a line of defense along the coasts of South Carolina, Georgia, and Florida. He arrived immediately after the capture of Port Royal by the Federal navy, and established his headquarters at Coosawhatchie, on the railroad, about midway between Charleston and Savannah. Beyond the prosecution of the work of. fortifying the cities and principal points on the coast and rivers, nothing of importance occurred during his three months' stay in this department. He was in Charleston at the time of the great conflagration, and was compelled to leave the Mills House, where he had taken rooms, and which was with great difficulty saved from destruction, and to take refuge in a private house on the " Battery."

In March, 1862, he returned to Richmond, and was assigned, on the 13th, under the direction of the President, to the conduct of the military operations of all the armies of

the Confederate States. This position was regarded by some
as rather anomalous in character, and yet there devolved
upon the general a great deal of work that did not appear on
the surface, and was of a kind not to be generally appreciated. Exercising a constant supervision over the condition
of affairs at each important point, thoroughly informed as to
the resources and necessities of the several commanders of
armies in the field, as well as of the dangers which respectively threatened them, he was enabled to give them wise
counsel, to offer them valuable suggestions, and to respond
to their demands for assistance and support to such extent as
the limited resources of the Government would permit. It
was in great measure due to his advice and encouragement
that General Magruder so stoutly and gallantly held his lines
on the Peninsula against General McClellan until troops
could be sent to his relief from General Johnston's army. I
recollect a telegraphic dispatch received by General Lee
from General Magruder, in which he stated that a council of
war which he had convened had unanimously determined
that his army should retreat; in reply to which General Lee
urged him to maintain his lines and to make as bold a front
as possible, and encouraged him with the prospect of being
early reënforced.

No better illustration of the nature and importance of
the duty performed by General Lee, while in this position,
can be given than the following letter—one of a number of
similar import—written by him to General Jackson, the
"rough" or original draft of which is still in my possession:

HEADQUARTERS, RICHMOND, VIRGINIA, *April* 29, 1862.

Major-General T. J. JACKSON, *commanding, etc., Swift Run Gap, Vir-*
    ginia.

GENERAL : I have had the honor to receive your letter
of yesterday's date. From the reports that reach me that are
entitled to credit, the force of the enemy opposite Fredericksburg is represented as too large to admit of any diminution
whatever of our army in that vicinity at present, as it might not

only invite an attack on Richmond, but jeopard the safety of the army in the Peninsula. I regret, therefore, that your request, to have five thousand men sent from that army to reënforce you, cannot be complied with. Can you draw enough from the command of General Edward Johnson to warrant you in attacking Banks ? The last return received from that army shows a present force of upward of thirty-five hundred, which, it is hoped, has been since increased by recruits and returned furloughs. As he does not appear to be pressed, it is suggested that a portion of his force might be temporarily removed from its present position, and made available for the movement in question. A decisive and successful blow at Banks's column would be fraught with the happiest results, and I deeply regret my inability to send you the reënforcements you ask. If, however, you think the combined forces of Generals Ewell and Johnson, with your own, inadequate for the move, General Ewell might, with the assistance of General Anderson's army near Fredericksburg, strike at McDowell's army between that city and Aquia, with much promise of success ; provided you feel sufficiently strong alone to hold Banks in check.

Very truly yours,   R. E. LEE.

The reader will observe that this letter bears the date "April 29, 1862." On the 5th or 6th of May General Jackson formed a junction between his own command and that of General Edward Johnson ; on the 8th of May he defeated Milroy at McDowell. Soon thereafter the command of General Ewell was united to that already under Jackson, and on the 25th of the same month Banks was defeated and put to flight.

Other incidents might be cited to illustrate this branch of the important service rendered at this period by General Lee. The line of earthworks around the city of Richmond, and other preparations for resisting an attack, testified to the immense care and labor bestowed upon the defense of the capital, so seriously threatened by the army of General McClellan.

On the last day of May the battle of Seven Pines, or Fair Oaks, was delivered, and General Johnston was wounded. On that afternoon the President and General Lee had gone out on the lines, and were present and under a severe fire as the troops of General Whiting went into action. Major-General G. W. Smith was next in rank to General Johnston, and assumed command of the army after the wounding of the latter. The next day, by order of the President, General Lee took personal command of the Army of Northern Virginia. He proceeded at once to make its position secure against attack, and to enhance its efficiency and strength, by every means in his power, so as to justify aggressive movements.

The brilliant achievements of the army under General Jackson, in the Shenandoah Valley, had so startled and paralyzed the Federal authorities, and had excited such fears for the safety of Washington, as to remove all apprehension of any immediate trouble from the enemy heretofore operating in the Valley, and to render improbable the junction of the army under McDowell with that of McClellan. General Lee, quick to observe and profit by the advantage to be derived from this propitious state of affairs, conceived the plan of drawing Jackson's command to his aid, swiftly and secretly, in order that he might, when thus reënforced, fall with all his strength upon the enemy's right flank, and compel him to a general engagement. The necessary orders were given. General Jackson moved with all possible celerity, and when he had reached Ashland, General Lee, having left Generals Magruder, Holmes, and Huger, with about twenty-eight thousand men, in the defenses of Richmond, on the 26th of June moved to the north side of the Chickahominy River with the remainder of his army, and took the initiative in the engagements embraced in the seven days' battles, from which resulted the complete discomfiture of the army under General McClellan, and its retreat to the protection of the fleet operating in James River.

Without attempting an account of any one of the severe engagements embraced in the seven days' battles, so fully described in General Lee's official report, I cannot forbear mention of a maladroit performance just before their termination, but for which I have always thought that McClellan's army would have been further driven, even "to the wall," and made to surrender—a trifling matter in itself apparently, and yet worthy of thoughtful consideration. General McClellan had retreated to Harrison's Landing; his army, supply and baggage trains were scattered in much confusion in and about Westover plantation ; our army was moving down upon him, its progress much retarded by natural and artificial obstacles ; General Stuart was in advance, in command of the cavalry. In rear of and around Westover there is a range of hills or elevated ground, completely commanding the plains below. Stuart, glorious Stuart! always at the front and full of fight, gained these hills. Below him, as a panorama, appeared the camps and trains of the enemy, within easy range of his artillery. The temptation was too strong to be resisted : he commanded some of his guns to open fire. The consternation caused thereby was immediate and positive. It frightened the enemy, but it enlightened him.

Those heights in our possession, the enemy's position was altogether untenable, and he was at our mercy ; unless they could be recaptured his capitulation was inevitable. Half a dozen shells from Stuart's battery quickly demonstrated this. The enemy, not slow in comprehending his danger, soon advanced his infantry in force, to dislodge our cavalry and repossess the heights. This was accomplished : the hills were fortified, and became the Federal line of defense, protected at either flank by a bold creek which emptied into James River, and by the heavy batteries of the fleet anchored opposite.[1] Had the infantry been up, General Lee would have

---

[1] "The retreat of the army from Malvern Hill to Harrison's Bar was very precipitate. The troops upon their arrival there were huddled together in great

made sure of this naturally strong line, fortified it well, maintained it against assault, and dictated to General Mc-Clellan terms of surrender; and had the attention of the enemy not been so precipitately directed to his danger by the shots from the little howitzers, it is reasonable to presume that the infantry would have been up in time to secure the plateau. The following extract from General Stuart's manuscript, "Reports and Notes on the War,"[1] gives more in detail the circumstances just related:

HEADQUARTERS CAVALRY, July 14, 1862.

. . . . I therefore sent down that night a howitzer toward Westover, under Captain Pelham, supported by Irving's squadron, First Virginia Cavalry, with orders to reach the immediate vicinity of the river-road below, so as to shell it if the enemy attempted to retreat that night. A squadron was left (Georgia Legion) near Shirley, and the main body bivouacked contiguous to oat-fields—of necessity our sole dependence for forage since leaving the White House; but the regiments were warned that the pursuit might be resumed at any moment during the night

confusion, the entire army being collected within a space of about three miles along the river. No orders were given the first day for occupying the height which commanded the position, nor were the troops so placed as to be able to resist an attack in force by the enemy; and nothing but a heavy rain, thereby preventing the enemy from bringing up their artillery, saved the army there from destruction. The enemy did succeed in bringing up some of their artillery, and threw some shells into the camp, before any preparations for defense had been made. On the 3d of July the heights were taken possession of by our troops, and works of defense commenced, and then, and not until then, was our army secure in that position."—Extract from the "Report of the Committee on the Conduct of the War" (U. S. Congress), Part I., p. 27.

General Casey testified as follows: "The enemy had come down with some artillery upon our army massed together on the river, the heights commanding the position not being in our possession. Had the enemy come down and taken possession of those heights with a force of twenty or thirty thousand men, they would, in my opinion, have taken the whole of our army, except that small portion of it that might have got off on the transports. I felt very much alarmed for the army until we had got possession of those heights, and fortified them. After that it was a strong position."—Ibid., p. 446.

[1] On file in the archives of the Southern Historical Society, Richmond, Va.

should Captain Pelham's reconnaissance apprise us of a continu-
ance of the retreat.

During the night Captain Pelham wrote to me that the
enemy had taken position between Shirley and Westover, nearer
the latter, and described the locality, the nature of Herring
Creek on the enemy's right, and indicated the advantage to be
gained by taking possession with artillery of Evelington Heights
— a plateau commanding completely the enemy's encamp-
ment. I forwarded this report at once to the commanding
general through General Jackson, and proceeded to the ground
with my command, except one regiment—the Ninth Virginia
Cavalry, Colonel W. H. F. Lee—which was ordered down the
road by Nance's shop, and thence across toward Charles City
Court-House, so as to extend my left, and keep a lookout
toward Forge Bridge, by which route I was liable to be attacked in flank and rear by Stoneman, should he endeavor a
junction by land with McClellan.

1 found Evelington Heights easily gained. A squadron in
possession vacated without much hesitation, retreating up the
road, the only route by which it could reach Westover, owing
to the impassability of Herring Creek below Roland's mill.
Colonel Martin was sent around farther to the left, and the
howitzer brought into action in the river-road, to fire upon the
enemy's camp. Judging from the great commotion and excitement caused below, it must have had considerable effect.
We soon had prisoners from various corps and divisions, and
from their statements, as well as those of citizens, I learned that
the enemy's main body was there, but much reduced and demoralized. I kept the commanding general apprised of my movements, and I soon learned from him that Longstreet and Jackson were *en route* to my support. I held the ground from about
9 A. M. until 2 P. M., when the enemy had contrived to get one
battery into position on this side the creek. The fire was, however, kept up until a body of infantry was found approaching
by our right flank. I had no apprehension, however, as I felt
sure Longstreet was near by; and, although Pelham reported
but two rounds of ammunition left, I held out, knowing how important it was to hold the ground until Longstreet arrived.

The enemy's infantry advanced, and the battery kept up its fire. I just then learned that Longstreet had taken the wrong road, and was at Nance's shop, six or seven miles off. Pelham fired his last round, and the sharp-shooters, strongly posted in the skirt of woods bordering the plateau, exhausted every cartridge, and had at last to retire; not, however, without teaching many a foeman the bitter lesson of death.

My command had been so cut off from sources of supply, and so constantly engaged with the enemy, that the abundant supply it began with on the 26th of June was entirely exhausted. I kept pickets at Bradley's store that night, and remained with my command on the west side of the creek near Phillip's farm. General Longstreet came up late in the evening; he had been led by his guide out of his proper route. The next day, July 4th, General Jackson's command drove in the enemy's advance-pickets.

I pointed out the position of the enemy, now occupying, apparently in force, the plateau from which I shelled their camp the day before, and showed him the route by which the plateau could be reached to the left, and submitted my plan for dispossessing the enemy and attacking his camp. This was subsequently laid before the commanding general.

The enemy's position had been well reconnoitred by Blackford, of the engineers, the day before, from a close view, and further on this day, July 4th, demonstrating that his position was strong, difficult to reach, except with rifled cannon, and completely flanked by gunboats—all which were powerful arguments, and no doubt had their due weight with the commanding general against renewing an attack, thus far of unbroken success, against a stronghold where the enemy had been reënforced beyond a doubt. . . .

It is most disingenuous to speak of the retreat of General McClellan's army as a "change of base" which that commander had purposed to make for some time previous to General Lee's attack. This has been claimed by certain writers, but his repeated dispatches to the authorities at Washington, the last bearing date the 25th of June, in which he signifies his intention to attack General Lee, completely refute the idea that his movements after General Lee's assaults were the carrying out of a preconceived determination to change his base of operations to the James River. His army was well in hand, and greatly outnumbered that of his antagonist; he had proposed to assume the offensive and bring on a "general engagement" on the very day that he was assailed;[1] after the first attack at Mechanicsville, when the purpose of General Lee was fully disclosed, he received the assaults of the latter on ground of his own selection; his men were protected to a greater or less extent by hastily-constructed but effective works—especially was this the case at Gaines's Mill, where Hood's command charged upon and captured one of the strongest positions ever assailed by either side during the entire war—and he destroyed large quantities of stores in his hurried movements to his "new base." In all this there is incontestable proof that he was fairly beaten and compelled to retreat. In this connection I submit the following extracts from the dispatches sent by General McClellan at that period to the President and the Secretary of War, and published in full in the "Report on the Conduct of the War," Part I., pages 327–340:

May 21, 1862.—. . . I believe there is a great struggle before this army, but I am neither dismayed nor discouraged. I wish to strengthen its force as much as I can; but, in any event, I shall fight it with all the skill and caution and determination that I possess. And I trust that the result may either obtain for me the permanent confidence of my Government, or that it may close my career.

June 2, 1862.—. . . The result is, that our left is within four miles of Richmond. I only wait for the river to fall, to cross with the rest of the force, and make a general attack. The *morale* of my troops is now such that I can venture much. I do not fear for odds against me. . . .

June 7, 1862.—. . . I shall be in perfect readiness to move

---

[1] General McClellan's report.

forward to take Richmond the moment that McCall reaches here and the ground will admit the passage of artillery. . . .

June 11, 1862.—McCall's troops have commenced arriving at White House. . . . Weather good to-day. . . . Give me a little good weather, and I shall have progress to report here.

June 12, 1862.— . . . Have moved headquarters across the Chickahominy. Weather now good; roads and ground rapidly drying.

June 14, 1862.—Weather now very favorable. I shall advance as soon as the bridges are completed and the ground fit for artillery to move.

June 18, 1862.— . . . A general engagement may take place any hour. An advance by us involves a battle more or less decisive. After to-morrow we shall fight the rebel army as soon as Providence will permit. We shall await only a favorable condition of the earth and sky, and the completion of some necessary preliminaries. . . .

June 25, 1862.—The rebel force is stated at two hundred thousand, including Jackson and Beauregard. I shall have to contend against vastly superior odds, if these reports be true; but this army will do all in the power of men to hold their position and repulse any attack. I regret my great inferiority of numbers, but feel that I am in no way responsible for it. . . . I will do all that a general can do with the splendid army I have the honor to command, and if it is destroyed by overwhelming numbers, can at least die with it and share its fate; but if the result of the action which will probably occur to-morrow or within a short time is a disaster, the responsibility cannot be thrown on my shoulders.

June 27, 1862, 10 A. M.—The troops on the other side are now well in hand, and the whole army so concentrated that it can take advantage of the first mistake made by the enemy. . . . White House yet undisturbed. Success of yesterday complete.

June 27, 1862, 12 M.—My change of position on other side just in time. Heavy attack now being made by Jackson and two other divisions. Expect attack also on this side.

June 27, 1862, 3 P. M.—We have been fighting nearly all day against greatly superior numbers. We shall endeavor to hold our own, and if compelled to fall back, shall do it in good order, upon James River if possible. Our men fight like veterans, and will do all that men can do. If we have to fall back on James River, supplies should be passed up to us, under protection of the gunboats, as rapidly as possible.

June 28, 1862, 12.20 A. M.—I now know the full history of the day. On this side of the river (the right bank) we repulsed several very strong attacks. On the left bank, our men did all that men could do—all that soldiers could accomplish; but they were overwhelmed by vastly superior numbers, even after I brought my last reserves into action. Had I twenty thousand or even ten thousand fresh troops to use to-morrow, I could take Richmond; but I have not a man in reserve, and shall be glad to cover my retreat and save the material and *personnel* of the army. If we have lost the day, we have yet preserved our honor, and no one need blush for the Army of the Potomac. I have lost this battle because my force was too small. . . . I still hope to retrieve our fortunes. . . . I know that a few thousand men more would have changed this battle from a defeat to a victory.

To this Mr. Lincoln replied:

June 28, 1862.— . . . Save your army at all events. . . .

From Haxall's plantation General McClellan telegraphed:

July 1, 1862.— . . . My men are completely exhausted, and I dread the result if we are attacked to-day by fresh troops. . . . I now pray for time. . . .

Mr. Lincoln to General McClellan:

July 1, 1862.— . . . If you are not strong enough to face the enemy, you must find a place of security and wait, rest and repair. Maintain your ground, if you can, but save the army at all events, even if you fall back to Fortress Monroe.

General McClellan to President Lincoln:

BERKELEY-HARRISON'S BAR, *July* 2, 1862, 5 P. M.

I have succeeded in getting this army to this place, on the banks of James River. . . .

I have not yielded an inch of ground unnecessarily, but have retired to prevent the superior force of the enemy from cutting me off, and to take a different base of operations.

In the testimony of General McClellan before the Committee on the Conduct of the War, the following appears:

Question. Did you suppose the enemy to be your superior in strength before the battle of Gaines's Mill?

Answer. My recollection is that I did.

Q. And did you suppose at that time that you would be obliged to retreat?

A. It was a contingency I thought of. But my impression is that, up to the time of the battle of Gaines's Mill, I still hoped that we should be able to hold our own.[1]

Colonel B. S. Alexander testified before the committee that—

While at headquarters, receiving his instructions (to proceed to James River with an escort to communicate with the gunboats, and order supplies to be brought up the river), he was shown a printed order, not then issued, directing the destruction of the baggage of officers and men, and the tents, camp-equipage, and things of that kind; appealing to the army to submit to this privation, as it would be only temporary—" only for a few days." He remonstrated with General McClellan against issuing such an order; that it would have a bad effect, would demoralize the army, as it would be telling them, more plainly than they could be told in any other way, that they were defeated, and running for their lives. The order was not issued, and General McClellan testifies that he has no recollection of any such order.[2]

From these extracts, I think it will be clear to the candid reader that the retreat to James River was a compulsory one, and due to a defeat then acknowledged by General McClellan himself.

The fighting, however, was not invariably attended with

[1] "Report on the Conduct of the War," Part I., p. 25.   [2] Ibid., Part I., p. 434.

success to the Confederates; notably, the defense of Malvern Hill by the Federals was in favor of the latter, which result was as much due to the mismanagement of the Confederate troops as to the naturally strong position occupied by the Federals and their gallantry in its defense.

Considerable delay was occasioned in the pursuit, from the fact that the ground was unknown to the Confederate commanders. On this occasion General Magruder took the wrong route, and had to be recalled, thereby losing much precious time ; and, when after serious and provoking delay the lines were formed for attack, there was some misunderstanding of the orders of the commanding general, and, instead of a spirited, united advance by the entire line, as contemplated, the divisions were moved forward at different times, each attacking independently, and each in turn repulsed. Moreover, owing to the peculiar character of the ground, artillery could not be advantageously placed to aid the assaulting columns; whereas the Federal batteries, strongly posted and most handsomely served, contributed in a very great degree to the successful stand made by McClellan's retreating army at Malvern Hill.

EFFECTIVE STRENGTH OF THE TWO ARMIES IN THE SEVEN DAYS' BATTLES.

A statement of the strength of the troops under General Johnston, now on file in the Archive-Office of the War Department, shows that on the 21st of May, 1862, he had present for duty:

Smith's division: consisting of the brigades of Whiting, Hood, Hampton, Hatton, and Pettigrew	10,592
Longstreet's division: consisting of the brigades of A. P. Hill, Pickett, R. H. Anderson, Wilcox, Colston, and Pryor	13,816
Magruder's division: consisting of the brigades of McLaws, Kershaw, Griffith, Cobb, Toombs, and D. R. Jones	15,680
D. H. Hill's division: consisting of the brigades of Early, Rodes, Raines, Featherston, and "the commands" of Colonels Ward and Crump	11,151
Cavalry brigade	1,289
Reserve artillery	1,160
Total effective of all arms	53,688

In addition to the troops above enumerated, there were two brigades subject to the orders of General Johnston, then stationed in the vicinity of Hanover Junction : one under the command of General J. R. Anderson, and the other under the command of General Branch ; they were subsequently incorporated into the division of General A. P. Hill, and participated in the battles around Richmond. I have no official data to determine the strength of these two brigades; that under General Branch was attacked by Porter's corps of McClellan's army, on the 27th of May, and suffered severely. General McClellan claims to have captured seven hundred and thirty prisoners and to have killed two hundred of Branch's command in that engagement. General Anderson informs me that the strength of his brigade in the seven days' battles was between two thousand and twenty-three hundred effective, and agrees with me in estimating the strength of the two brigades at that time at four thousand effective.

Subsequent to the date of the return of the army around Richmond heretofore given, but previous to the battle of Seven Pines, General Johnston was reënforced by General Huger's division, consisting of three brigades, under Generals Mahone, Armistead, and Wright. In the bound volume of the "Reports of the Operations of the Army of Northern Virginia" (vol. i., pp. 371–385), I find that Mahone's strength at the commencement of the battles around Richmond was eighteen hundred; Wright's, two thousand; Armistead's, twelve hundred and eight, present for duty. Total of Huger's division, five thousand and eight effective.

If the strength of the five brigades just enumerated be added to the return of the 21st of May, we shall have sixty-two thousand six hundred and ninety-six as the effective strength of the army under General Johnston on the 31st of May, 1862.[1]

---

[1] As my purpose is to ascertain the strength of General Lee's army in the battles around Richmond, I put Huger's strength at that time in this estimate.

Deduct the losses sustained in the battle of Seven Pines, as shown by the official reports of casualties, say six thousand and eighty-four,[1] and we have fifty-six thousand six hundred and twelve as the effective strength of the army when General Lee assumed the command.

Previous to the seven days' battles the following reenforcements reached General Lee:

Ripley's brigade, officially reported as twenty-three hundred and sixty-six strong.[2]

Holmes's command, embracing the brigades of Ransom, Walker, Daniel, and Wise, and a small force of artillery and cavalry. In his official report, General Ransom puts five of his six regiments at three thousand effective.[3] Allowing the average strength of the reported five for the excluded sixth, viz., six hundred, and it would give thirty-six hundred as his total effective strength. In General Holmes's report[4] he states the strength of Walker's brigade as thirty-six hundred; that of Daniel's, as fifteen hundred and seventy; that of Wise, as seven hundred and fifty-two. Besides the infantry, there were six batteries of artillery (four hundred and forty-three effective), and a battalion of cavalry (one hundred and thirty strong). The total effective of Holmes's command, including Ransom's brigade, was, therefore, ten thousand and ninety-five—say ten thousand men.

Lawton's brigade, the last reënforcement received, was thirty-five hundred strong, as by the official report of its commander.[5]

The result would be the same, though the method would be different, if I took the strength of the three brigades on the 21st of May and deducted their losses previous to the battles around Richmond; as I have not this information, I adopt the other method.

[1] Longstreet's loss was four thousand eight hundred and fifty-one, including that sustained by D. H. Hill's division.—" Southern Historical Society Papers," vol. i., p. 415.

G. W. Smith's loss was twelve hundred and thirty-three.—General Johnston's " Narrative," p. 140.

[2] " Reports of the Operations of the Army of Northern Virginia under General Lee; published by Authority of the Comfederate Congress," vol. i., p. 234.

[3] Ibid., p. 368.   [4] Ibid., p. 151.   [5] Ibid., p. 270.

The commands just enumerated include all the reën-forcements received by General Lee, except the command of General Jackson, brought from the Valley. This consisted of two divisions, viz.: Jackson's old division, embracing three brigades, commanded respectively by General Win-der and Colonels Cunningham and Fulkerson; and Ewell's division, embracing the brigades of Elzey, Trimble, and Sey-mour. These two divisions were very much reduced by reason of the active campaign in the Valley. Of Jackson's old division, we have the effective strength of one of its three brigades, before it marched to join General Lee, viz., that under Winder, which was officially reported eleven hundred and thirty-five strong.[1] Taking this as an average, the divis-ion had an effective strength of thirty-four hundred and five. Of Ewell's division, one brigade—and that the largest—viz., Elzey's, numbered twelve hundred and ninety-three,[2] when Jackson's command joined General Lee. Taking that as an average, the division numbered thirty-eight hundred and seventy-nine effective. Add one thousand men for the regi-ment of cavalry, and the artillery which accompanied Gen-eral Jackson, and we have eight thousand two hundred and eighty-four as the total effective of his command.

For the purpose of deceiving the enemy, two brigades under Whiting—viz., his own and Hood's—were sent to the Valley to join General Jackson just before he moved to re-enforce General Lee. For the same reason, General Law-ton's brigade, on reaching Virginia when on the way to join General Lee, was in like manner diverted. Having already counted these brigades, I do not estimate them in giving the strength of General Jackson's command.

We have now seen that when General Lee assumed the command of the Army of Northern Virginia its strength was fifty-six thousand six hundred and twelve; and that he was subsequently reënforced by Ripley's brigade, numbering

[1] "Report of Operations around Richmond," p. 70.
[2] Ibid., "Early's Report," p. 303; and Elzey's "Brigade Casualties," p. 142.

twenty-three hundred and sixty-six men; Holmes's command, ten thousand strong; Lawton's brigade, thirty-five hundred; and Jackson's two divisions, eight thousand two hundred and eighty-four: making the total of reënforcements received twenty-four thousand one hundred and fifty; which would make eighty thousand seven hundred and sixty-two as the effective strength of the army under General Lee, in the seven days' battles around Richmond.[1]

When General Lee assumed command of the army it was organized into divisions and brigades, as follows:

Longstreet's division—six brigades, viz.: Pickett's, R. H. Anderson's, Wilcox's, Kemper's, Pryor's, and Featherston's.

A. P. Hill's division—six brigades, viz.: J. R. Anderson's, Gregg's, Field's, Pender's, Branch's, and Archer's.

D. H. Hill's division—four brigades, viz.: Rodes's, G. B. Anderson's, Garland's, and Colquitt's.

Magruder's command—six brigades, viz.: Semmes's, Kershaw's, Griffith's, Cobb's, Toombs's, and D. R. Jones's. These were organized into three divisions of two brigades each, under Generals Magruder, McLaws, and D. R. Jones.

Huger's division—three brigades, viz.: Mahone's, Armistead's, and Wright's.

Whiting's division—two brigades, viz.: his own, under Colonel Law, and Hood's.

In all, there were twenty-seven brigades.

The army under General Lee in the battles around Richmond embraced the following commands:

Longstreet's division—six brigades, viz.: Pickett's, Anderson's, Wilcox's, Kemper's, Pryor's, and Featherston's.

A. P. Hill's division — six brigades, viz.: Anderson's, Gregg's, Field's, Pender's, Branch's, and Archer's.

D. H. Hill's division—five brigades, viz.: Rodes's, Garland's, Anderson's, Colquitt's, and Ripley's.

[1] General Early, in a very exhaustive article on this subject, published in the "Southern Historical Society Papers," vol. i., p. 407, puts General Lee's strength "under eighty thousand effective."

Magruder's command—six brigades, viz.: Semmes's, Kershaw's, Griffith's, Cobb's, Toombs's, and D. R. Jones's.

Huger's division—three brigades, viz.: Mahone's, Armistead's, and Wright's.

Whiting's division — two brigades, viz. : his own and Hood's.

Jackson's division—three brigades, viz.: Winder's, Cunningham's, and Fulkerson's.

Ewell's division—three brigades, viz.: Elzey's, Trimble's, and Seymour's.

Holmes's command—four brigades, viz.: Walker's, Ransom's, Daniel's, and Wise's.

Lawton's brigade—unattached, under General Jackson's command.

In all, thirty-nine brigades.

General Lee had received, then, but twelve brigades additional after he assumed command of the army. These, as has already been shown, were Ripley's, Walker's, Ransom's, Daniel's, Wise's, Lawton's, and the six brought by General Jackson from the Valley.

By reference to the official reports of the division commanders of the operations of their respective commands in the battles around Richmond, I find the following concerning the number of troops employed in those operations:

General Holmes puts his command, exclusive of Ransom's brigade, at six thousand infantry and six batteries of artillery numbering four hundred and forty-three men;[1] General Ransom's brigade, as already shown, numbered thirty-six hundred;[2] thus Holmes's entire command amounted to ten thousand men. General Magruder reports his strength as thirteen thousand.[3] General Huger's—excluding Ransom's brigade, temporarily attached and already estimated—as shown by the reports of his brigade commanders, was five thousand.[4] Gen-

---

[1] "Reports of the Operations of the Army of Northern Virginia," vol. i., p. 151.

[2] Ibid., p. 368.   [3] Ibid., p. 190.   [4] Ibid., pp. 371–385.

eral A. P. Hill gives his strength as fourteen thousand.[1] General D. H. Hill puts his at ten thousand.[2] General Lawton gives the strength of his brigade as thirty-five hundred.[3] General Longstreet does not state the strength of his division, but General E. P. Alexander, his chief of artillery, quoting from the official records of Longstreet's command, puts the strength of the division in the seven days' battles at nine thousand and fifty-one.[4] General Whiting does not give his strength, but the two brigades on the 21st of May, 1862, numbered four thousand three hundred and twenty;[5] they lost pretty heavily at Seven Pines or Fair Oaks, and on the 20th of July, 1862, numbered but thirty-eight hundred and fifty-two;[6] it is fair to estimate them, therefore, on the 26th of June, 1862, at four thousand. General Jackson does not give the strength of his two divisions, but I have already adduced good testimony to prove that his command, excluding Whiting and Lawton, did not exceed eight thousand two hundred and eighty-four. Allowing four thousand for the cavalry and the reserve artillery—nearly double what it was a month previous—and there results a total of all arms of eighty thousand eight hundred and thirty-five. This confirms the estimate obtained by my first method.

It appears from the official returns of the Army of the Potomac (as given by Mr. Swinton, in his history of that army), that, on the 20th of June, 1862, General McClellan had present for duty one hundred and fifteen thousand one hundred and two.[7] Mr. Swinton also states that General McClellan reached the James River with "between eighty-five and ninety thousand men," and that the Federal loss, in the seven days' battles, was fifteen thousand two hundred and forty-nine; this would make the army one hundred and five thousand strong at the commencement of the battles.

[1] Ibid., p. 173. [2] Ibid., p. 187. [3] Ibid., p. 270.
[4] "Southern Historical Society Papers."
[5] "Return of the Army under General Johnston," Archive-Office, United States War Department, see chapter xiv.
[6] "Return of the Army of Northern Virginia," chapter xiv.
[7] For copy of "Return of the Army of the Potomac," see also "Report on the Conduct of the War," Part I., p. 337.

I presume that the difference of ten thousand between this statement and the official returns is explained by the fact that no account is taken of General Dix's corps of nine thousand two hundred and seventy-seven effective, stationed at Fort Monroe, but under General McClellan's command and embraced in the returns of his army. The force under General McClellan, however, appears to shrink as we study this question, for the same author says (page 151), " On the north side of the Chickahominy thirty thousand Union troops were being assailed by seventy thousand Confederates, and twenty-five thousand Confederates on the south side held in check sixty thousand Union troops." The entire strength of General McClellan's army, according to this last statement, would be but ninety thousand. This is evidently an under-estimate of the Federal strength; and while the Confederate force on the south side, as here given, is nearly accurate, that on the north side is excessive by at least seventeen thousand. There remained on the south side of the Chickahominy, of Lee's army, the commands of Holmes, Magruder, and Huger; their effective strength on the 26th of June was about twenty-eight thousand, as shown by the reports of these officers of the operations of their commands in the seven days' battles.

The difference between this and eighty-one thousand would give fifty-three thousand as the strength of the Confederate force—infantry, artillery, and cavalry—under General Lee, operating in the flank movement on the north side of the Chickahominy. If we adopt as correct the Confederate loss as given by Mr. Swinton, viz., nineteen thousand, it would then appear that when McClellan reached the river with "eighty-five or ninety thousand men,"[1] he was being pursued by General Lee with but sixty-two thousand.

[1] *See* General McClellan's testimony, "Report on the Conduct of the War," Part I., p. 437.

CHAPTER VI.

General Lee manœuvres to effect the Withdrawal of General McClellan's Army. —Jackson engages Pope at Cedar Run, or Slaughter's Mountain.—Removal of the Federal Army from James River.—The Second Battle of Manassas.— The First Invasion.—Operations in Maryland.—McClellan in Possession of Lee's Order of Battle.—Boonesboro, or South Mountain.—Capture of Harper's Ferry by Jackson's Forces.—Battle of Sharpsburg.—General Lee retires to Virginia.—Incidents illustrating the Devotion to Duty and Great Self-Control of the Confederate Leader.

ALTHOUGH defeated, the army under General McClellan was still a formidable force, and was being constantly strengthened. Its proximity to the Confederate capital, and its unassailable position, the facility with which it could be transferred across James River for operations on the south side, the capacity of the North indefinitely to recruit its ranks, and of the Government to repair and increase its equipment, rendered the situation one of profound solicitude, and presented to the Confederate commander the alternative of remaining a passive observer of his adversary's movements, or of devising a campaign which would compel the withdrawal of the hostile army from its position of constant menace.

With a just conception of the inordinate fear which possessed the mind of the Federal civil authorities for the safety of their capital, he concluded that seriously to threaten that city, either by strategic manœuvres or by a decisive blow struck at the army in its front, would be the surest way of effecting the removal of McClellan's army from its position on James River.

With this view he sent General Jackson in advance with his two divisions, followed by that of A. P. Hill, to engage General Pope, who commanded the Federal army in Northern Virginia, intending, as soon as his anticipations of the effect of this move were realized, to follow promptly with the bulk of his army.

In vindication of his sagacity, information was soon received of the transfer of troops from McClellan's army on James River to Washington.

Leaving two divisions of infantry and a brigade of cavalry at Richmond, he now moved with the rest of the army to join General Jackson, who had already presented a rebel front to the astonished gaze of Major-General John Pope, unaccustomed to such a sight, and had commenced at Cedar Run, on the 9th of August, that series of brilliant manœuvres and engagements which so dazed the Federal commander, and so startled and alarmed the authorities at Washington.

These movements culminated with a decisive victory for the Confederates, under General Lee, over the army under General Pope, on the plains of Manassas, on the 30th of August. In the series of engagements, " more than seven thousand prisoners were taken, in addition to about two thousand wounded left in our hands. Thirty pieces of artillery, upward of twenty thousand stand of small-arms, numerous colors, and a large amount of stores, besides those taken by General Jackson at Manassas Junction, were captured." [1]

Vanquished at Manassas, General Pope next essayed to make a stand in the fortified lines about Centreville; but another *détour* by General Jackson, under General Lee's orders, caused a further retreat in the direction of Washington, and in the early days of September the Federal army—now embracing the combined forces of McClellan and Pope—was retired within the line of fortifications constructed on the Virginia side of the river, for the protection of the Federal capital.

[1] Extract from General Lee's " Report," p. 24.

Barely three months had elapsed since General Lee took the field, and, behold! the position of the two hostile armies, with relation to their respective seats of government, was completely reversed; fortunately for that of the North, a wide and impassable river lay between it and the victorious army of the South.

With the battles of Cedar Run, or Slaughter's Mountain, and (second) Manassas, two more victories were recorded for Confederate arms, and another Federal general was added to the list of the discomfited.

The career of General Pope was as brief and remarkable, when contrasted with his blustering proclamations, as the movements of Generals Lee and Jackson, in bringing it to a grievous termination, were audacious and brilliant.

STRENGTH OF THE OPPOSING ARMIES IN THE BATTLES OF
CEDAR RUN AND (SECOND) MANASSAS.

The field-return of the "Department of Northern Virginia" of the 20th of July, 1862, shows a total "present for duty" in that department of sixty-nine thousand five hundred and fifty-nine. Of this number the Army of Northern Virginia embraced but fifty-seven thousand three hundred and twenty-eight. The remaining twelve thousand two hundred and thirty-one were serving south of James River, and in North Carolina, and were included in the departmental returns, because that section of country was then comprised within the territorial limits of the department under the command of General Lee. This return, however, did not include Jackson's command, consisting of his own and Ewell's divisions, then near Gordonsville. The movements of these two divisions doubtless had prevented their making the formal returns usually required. Their effective strength could not have exceeded eight thousand.[1] Jackson was

---

[1] This estimate allows this division as much as it had in the seven days' battles.

reënforced by A. P. Hill, early in August, whose division in the field-return of the 20th of July, mentioned above, showed, as " present for duty," ten thousand six hundred and twenty-three ; so that, with this reënforcement, General Jackson had available at the battle of Cedar Run eighteen thousand six hundred and twenty-three men. At that time General Pope had available the three corps of Banks, McDowell, and Si-gel, numbering forty-three thousand men, according to his statement ;[1] but only Banks's corps and one division of Mc-Dowell's corps were engaged.

When General Lee moved forward to join General Jackson he took with him the divisions of Longstreet, D. R. Jones, Hood, and Anderson, leaving in front of Richmond the divisions of D. H. Hill and McLaws, and two brigades under J. G. Walker.

A portion of the cavalry under General Stuart accompanied General Lee, leaving a brigade under General Hampton in front of Richmond.

The total present for duty of the cavalry arm of the service on the 20th of July was four thousand and thirty-five ; probably fifteen hundred remained with Hampton, and twenty-five hundred accompanied General Lee. The present for duty in the artillery of the same date was thirty-two hundred and fifty-two ; of this number certainly not over twenty-five hundred accompanied General Lee.

Besides the troops embraced in the return of the 20th of July, there were two brigades (Drayton's and Evans's) recently arrived from South Carolina, which joined General Lee previous to the battle. In a letter dated June 9, 1874, Major Henry E. Young, subsequently on the staff of the commanding general, but then adjutant-general of Drayton's brigade, and also of the division composed of these two brigades, during its temporary command by General Drayton, states that the strength of the two brigades did not exceed

---

[1] General Pope's " Report," " Report on the Conduct of the War," Part II., Supplement, p. 109.

four thousand six hundred present for duty.[1] Assuming this estimate to be correct, and taking the strength of the other commands as given on the return of the 20th of July, we have the following as the army under General Lee in the series of engagements that terminated with the second battle of Manassas :

Jackson's three divisions, as heretofore given		18,623
Less casualties in battle of Cedar Run (Jackson's official report)		1,314
		17,309
Longstreet's command—viz.: his own division	8,486	
Hood's "	3,852	
Jones's "	3,713	
		16,051
Anderson's division		6,117
Drayton's and Evans's brigades		4,600
Total infantry		44,077
Cavalry (as estimated above)		2,500
Artillery "		2,500
Total of all arms		49,077

At the opening of the campaign, General Pope had under his command in the field the three army-corps of Generals Sigel, Banks, and McDowell, numbering, according to the official returns, forty-seven thousand eight hundred and seventy-eight effective, as follows: First Army-Corps (Sigel's), eleven thousand four hundred and ninety-eight infantry and artillery; Second Army-Corps (Banks's), fourteen thousand five hundred and sixty-seven infantry and artillery; Third Army-Corps (McDowell's), eighteen thousand five hundred and seventy-five infantry and artillery; cavalry, eight thousand seven hundred and thirty-eight; total, fifty-three thousand three hundred and seventy-eight, from which deduct detached commands and cavalry unfit for service six

[1] General Sorrel, the adjutant-general of Longstreet's command, puts the strength of these brigades at four thousand five hundred when they marched from Gordonsville in 1862, just previous to the battle of Manassas. They were at that time made a part of General Longstreet's command.

thousand five hundred, and there remains forty-seven thousand eight hundred and seventy-eight effective.[1]

Only Banks's corps, and Rickett's division of McDowell's corps, were engaged at the battle of Cedar Run, or Slaughter's Mountain. General Pope estimates his loss in that engagement, in killed, wounded, and missing, at eighteen hundred.[2]

General Pope then received the following reënforcements: on the 14th of August, Reno's corps of Burnside's army; on the 23d of August, Reynolds's division of Pennsylvania Reserves; and on the 26th and 27th of August, the corps of Heintzelman and Porter, of the Army of the Potomac.

In his report, General Pope puts these reënforcements at twenty-eight thousand five hundred, as follows: Reno's corps, eight thousand; Reynolds's division, twenty-five hundred; Heintzelman's and Porter's corps, eighteen thousand.[3] This would make his aggregate effective strength, previous to the second battle of Manassas, seventy-six thousand three hundred and seventy-eight; and, deducting the losses at Cedar Run, eighteen hundred, we have seventy-four thousand five hundred and seventy-eight as his total available force in the series of engagements which terminated with his defeat near Groveton—(second) Manassas—on the 30th of August.

In this enumeration no mention is made of Sturgis, Cox, or Franklin. A portion of Cox's division was engaged at Manassas Junction, on the 27th of August; and Taylor's brigade of Franklin's division was defeated by the Confederates later on the same day, at the same place.

---

[1] Official return of the Army of Virginia of July 31, 1862; General Pope's "Report," "Report on the Conduct of the War," Part II., Supplement, p. 118. It is proper to state that General Pope disputes the correctness of the return of Banks's corps. In regard to this he says (p. 117): "Although I several times called General Bank's attention to the discrepancy between this return and the force he afterward stated to me he had led to the front, that discrepancy has never been explained, and I do not yet understand how General Banks could have been so greatly mistaken as to the force under his immediate command."

[2] Pope's "Report," p. 122.   [3] Ibid., pp. 122, 172.

Although I have adopted General Pope's figures (with the exception of Banks's strength already referred to, where I followed the official return of General Banks), I cannot reconcile his statement of the reënforcements received with the other official data before me. He estimates the troops received from the Army of the Potomac, previous to the battle, viz., Heintzelman's corps, Porter's corps, and Reynolds's division, at twenty thousand five hundred; he also puts the combined strength of Sumner's and Franklin's corps, which joined him after the battle, at nineteen thousand.

He thus makes it appear that all of McClellan's army, except Keyes's corps and Dix's corps, numbered but thirty-nine thousand five hundred men, although he speaks of that army as the "ninety-one thousand veteran troops from Harrison's Landing." The two corps of Keyes and Dix, and the cavalry, could hardly account for the difference of fifty-one thousand five hundred.

On the 20th of July, 1862, less than one month before the removal of the Army of the Potomac from the Peninsula, the official return [1] of that army showed present for duty one hundred and one thousand six hundred and ninety-one men, as follows:

Engineer brigade, cavalry division, provost-guard, etc......	8,735
Second Corps, General Sumner.........................	16,952
Third Corps, General Heintzelman......................	16,276
Fourth Corps, General Keyes...........................	14,490
Fifth Corps, General Porter............................	21,077
Sixth Corps, General Franklin.........................	14,014
Seventh Corps, General Dix........................... .	9,997
United States Signal Corps............................	150
	101,691

General Dix remained at Fortress Monroe. General Keyes with his corps covered the embarkation at Yorktown; all the rest were moved to reënforce General Pope. General

[1] "Report on the Conduct of the War," Part I., p. 344.

McClellan, having dispatched his corps successively at and near Fortress Monroe, followed with his staff on the 23d of August, and arrived at Aquia Creek the next day.

It will be seen that the combined strength of the Second and Sixth Corps (Sumner's and Franklin's) was thirty thousand nine hundred and sixty-six previous to the removal from the Peninsula to the front of Washington. When these two corps moved out to join General Pope, they numbered twenty-five thousand infantry,[1] although he only puts them at nineteen thousand. The combined strength of the Third and Fifth Corps (Heintzelman's and Porter's), on the 20th July, was thirty-seven thousand three hundred and fifty-three; and, assuming that the proportion of infantry in these corps was the same as in the Second and Sixth, their strength at Manassas should have been near thirty thousand. Porter's corps alone embraced between twenty and thirty regiments, and eight batteries of artillery,[2] and two weeks later, September 12th, numbered twenty thousand.[3]

McCall's division of Pennsylvania Reserves numbered on the 15th of June, 1862, nine thousand five hundred and fourteen effective;[4] its losses in the battles around Richmond were officially reported at three thousand and seventy-four,[5] so that it must have numbered about six thousand five hundred when it left the Peninsula to join General Pope, yet the latter reports this division but twenty-five hundred strong when it reached him.

Mr. Swinton, the author previously quoted, who enjoyed

[1] *See* General McClellan's dispatches, " Report on the Conduct of the War," Part I. " Sumner has about fourteen thousand infantry, without cavalry or artillery, here " (August 28, 1862, p. 461).

" Franklin has only between ten thousand and eleven thousand ready for duty " (August 29, 1862, p. 462).

[2] General McDowell's testimony, "Report on the Conduct of the War," Part II., Supplement, p. 175.

[3] " Report on the Conduct of the War," Part I., p. 39.

[4] Ibid., Part I., p. 345.

[5] From official report of casualties in the Army of the Potomac, " The American Conflict," p. 168.

unusual facilities for obtaining accurate information in all matters pertaining to the Federal army, states in his "Campaign of the Army of the Potomac" that the force under General Pope, before he received any reënforcements, was "near fifty thousand men." He also states (p. 179) that McDowell's corps, Sigel's corps, and Reynolds's (McCall's) division of Pennsylvania Reserves, on the 28th of August, made together " a force of forty thousand men." If we add to this Banks's corps, Reno's corps, and the two corps of Heintzelman and Porter, it would appear that on the 28th of August General Pope must have had an available force of seventy-five or eighty thousand men.

On the morning of the 30th of August—the decisive day—after deducting the losses incurred in the engagements of the 27th, 28th, and 29th, General Pope reports his effective strength as follows : [1] McDowell's corps, including Reynolds's division, twelve thousand ; Sigel's corps, seven thousand ; Reno's corps, seven thousand ; Heintzelman's corps, seven thousand ; Porter's corps, twelve thousand ; Banks's corps, five thousand : total, fifty thousand. At no time in his operations against General Pope had General Lee so many men.

In addition to the troops enumerated above, the divisions of Sturgis and Cox, and the corps of Sumner and Franklin, were within an easy march of General Pope, but only joined him after his retreat to Centreville. Sturgis's division numbered ten thousand ; Cox's division, seven thousand. [2] I have already given the strength of Sumner's and Franklin's corps. From first to last there must have been, according to the official returns, not less than one hundred and twenty thousand men in front of Washington to resist General Lee's advance. General Pope puts his strength on the 1st of September at Centreville, after the fighting was over, at sixty-three thousand men. His losses in killed and wounded were

[1] General Pope's " Report," p. 156.   [2] Ibid., p. 139.

very heavy, but his "missing" must have been enormous to account for this difference.[1]

Immediately after the victory of second Manassas, the Potomac was crossed, and the army under General Lee entered Maryland; Generals D. H. Hill and McLaws, who were left at Richmond, having been meanwhile directed to join the main army.

At Frederick City, information reached General Lee of the purpose of President Davis to follow in the rear of and join the army. To prevent a step so full of personal danger to the President, for the scouting and marauding parties of the enemy's cavalry were active in our rear, I was dispatched to meet him and dissuade him from carrying out such intention; and I did not rejoin the army until the night previous to the battle of Sharpsburg.

At this time General Lee conceived his plan of operations, embracing the capture of Harper's Ferry, and a subsequent concentration of the army to join issue in a grand battle with General McClellan, who had again vaulted into the headquarters-saddle of the Federal army, vacated by General Pope.

An order of battle was issued, stating in detail the position and duty assigned to each command of the army. General Jackson was to undertake the reduction and capture of Harper's Ferry, and had assigned to him for this purpose his own two divisions, and those of A. P. Hill, Anderson, and McLaws. Longstreet's two divisions, under Jones and Hood, and D. H. Hill's division, remained to hold in check the army under McClellan pending Jackson's operations.

It was the custom to send copies of such orders, marked "confidential," to the commanders of separate corps or di-

---

[1] "It is proper for me to state here, and I do it with regret and reluctance, that at least one-half of this great diminution of our forces was occasioned by skulking and straggling from the army. The troops which were brought into action fought with gallantry and determination, but thousands of men straggled away from their commands, and were not in any action."—General Pope's "Report," p. 164.

visions only, and to place the address of such separate commander in the bottom left-hand corner of the sheet containing the order. General D. H. Hill was in command of a division which had not been attached to nor incorporated with
either of the two wings of the Army of Northern Virginia. A
copy of the order was, therefore, in the usual course, sent to
him. After the evacuation of Frederick City by our forces,
a copy of General Lee's order was found in a deserted camp
by a soldier, and was soon in the hands of General McClellan. This copy of the order, it was stated at the time, was
addressed to " General D. H. Hill, commanding division."
General Hill has assured me that it could not have been his
copy, because he still has the original order received by him
in his possession. It is impossible, therefore, to explain how
a copy addressed to General D. H. Hill was thus carelessly
handled and lost.[1]

But what an advantage did this fortuitous event give the
Federal commander, whose heretofore snail-like movements
were wonderfully accelerated when he was made aware of
the fact of the division of our army, and of the small portion thereof which confronted him![2]

The God of battles alone knows what would have occurred
but for the singular accident mentioned; it is useless to
speculate on this point, but certainly the loss of this battle-
order constitutes one of the pivots on which turned the
event of the war.

Notwithstanding this unfortunate circumstance, the stubborn and heroic defense of the South Mountain Pass by

[1] Colonel Venable, one of my associates on the staff of General Lee, says in
regard to this matter: "This is very easily explained. One copy was sent
directly to Hill from headquarters. General Jackson sent him a copy, as he
regarded Hill in his command. It is Jackson's copy, in his own handwriting,
which General Hill has. The other was undoubtedly left carelessly by some
one at Hill's quarters."

[2] "Upon learning the contents of this order, I at once gave orders for a vigorous pursuit."—General McClellan's testimony, "Report on the Conduct of
the War," Part I., p. 440.

Longstreet and D. H. Hill, and Jackson's complete success
at Harper's Ferry, including the gallant resistance made at
Crampton's Gap by portions of McLaws's and Anderson's
commands [1] against the assaults of Franklin's corps, enabled
General Lee to unite his forces at Sharpsburg in time to
give battle, on the 17th of September, to his old adversary ;
but under altogether different circumstances from such as
were anticipated. Longstreet and D. H. Hill [2] in resisting
the assaults of the bulk of McClellan's army had suffered
very heavily. Jackson had been compelled, after considerable fighting, to hasten from Harper's Ferry (which place
was surrendered to him on the 15th), by forced marches of
extraordinary character, to join General Lee, who had remained with Longstreet. The route from Harper's Ferry
was strewed with foot-sore and weary men, too feeble to keep
up with the stronger and more active ; and, instead of going
into battle with full ranks, the brigades were but as regiments, and in some cases no stronger than a full company.

After the affair at South Mountain, the commands of
Longstreet and Hill were retired to Sharpsburg, and were
confronted on the 15th by McClellan's army, along the line
of Antietam Creek, but were not seriously attacked until
the next day.

[1] Cobb's and Semmes's brigades of McLaws's division, and Mahone's brigade
of Anderson's division.

[2] The resistance made by General D. H. Hill at South Mountain deserves
more than a passing notice. On the 14th of September, with the brigades of
Rodes, Garland, Colquitt, Anderson, and Ripley, numbering in the aggregate
less than five thousand men, for six or seven hours he successfully resisted
the repeated assaults of two corps of the army under General McClellan
(Burnside's and Hooker's), fully thirty thousand strong. About 3 P. M. he was
reënforced by the brigades of Drayton and Anderson, numbering nineteen
hundred men, and later in the day was joined by General Longstreet, with the
brigades of Evans, Pickett, Kemper, Jenkins, Hood, and Whiting ; only four of
these, however, numbering about three thousand men, became seriously engaged,
and they not until dusk. Thus it will be seen that a force of less than ten
thousand men held McClellan in check for an entire day.—" Reports of the Operations of the Army of Northern Virginia," p. 112 ; " Report on the Conduct
of the War," Part I., p. 640.

On the afternoon of the 16th General McClellan directed an attack by Hooker's corps on the Confederate left— Hood's two brigades—and during the whole of the 17th the battle was waged, with varying intensity, along the entire line. When the issue was first joined, on the afternoon of the 16th, General Lee had with him less than eighteen thousand men,[1] consisting of the commands of Longstreet and D. H. Hill, the two divisions of Jackson, and two brigades under Walker. Couriers were sent to the rear to hurry up the divisions of A. P. Hill, Anderson, and McLaws, hastening from Harper's Ferry, and these several commands, as they reached the front at intervals during the day, on the 17th, were immediately deployed and put to work. Every man was engaged. We had no reserve.

The fighting was heaviest and most continuous on the Confederate left. It is established upon indisputable Federal evidence that the three corps of Hooker, Mansfield, and Sumner, were completely shattered in the repeated but fruitless efforts to turn this flank, and two of these corps were rendered useless for further aggressive movements.[2] The

[1] The command of General Longstreet consisted of the six brigades under General D. R. Jones, viz., Kemper, Pickett, Jenkins, George Anderson, Drayton, and Toombs, numbering, according to General Jones's official report, twenty-four hundred and thirty men; two brigades under General Hood, numbering twenty-three hundred and thirty-two effective; and Evans's brigade, fifteen hundred strong; making Longstreet's total effective on the morning of the 16th of September six thousand two hundred and sixty-two. General D. H. Hill reports that he had but three thousand infantry in line of battle. General Jackson's command, by the official report of the division commanders, is shown to have been but five thousand strong. The command of General Walker consisted of his own brigade and that of General R. Ransom. I am informed by the latter that the brigades numbered about sixteen hundred effective each, making thirty-two hundred for the two. It will thus be seen that the total effective infantry in line of battle on the 16th was but seventeen thousand four hundred and sixty-two.

[2] "General Hooker's corps was dispersed; there is no question about that. I sent one of my staff-officers to find where they were, and General Ricketts, the only officer we could find, said that he could not raise three hundred men of his corps.

"There were some troops lying down on the left, which I took to belong to

aggregate strength of the attacking columns at this point reached forty thousand men,[1] not counting the two divisions of Franklin's corps, sent at a late hour in the day to rescue the Federal right from the impending danger of being itself destroyed; while the Confederates, from first to last, had less than fourteen thousand men on this flank, consisting of Jackson's two divisions, McLaws's division, and the two small divisions, of two brigades each, under Hood and Walker, with which to resist their fierce and oft-repeated assaults.

As a wall of adamant the fourteen thousand received the shock of the forty thousand; and the latter, staggered by the blow, reeled and recoiled in great disorder.

The disproportion in the centre and on our right was as great as, or even more decided than, on our left.

Indeed, the drawn battle of Sharpsburg was as forcible an illustration of Southern valor and determination as was furnished during the whole period of the war, when the great disparity in numbers between the two armies is considered.

From such informal reports as were received at the time, and from my own observation and knowledge, I estimated the effective strength of the Confederate army at Sharpsburg at thirty-seven thousand men—twenty-nine thousand infantry and eight thousand cavalry and artillery.

But I am now satisfied, after reference to the official reports of the Maryland campaign, published by authority of the Confederate Congress, that my estimate was excessive. Fortunately, these reports are explicit, and enable me to determine, with almost absolute certainty, the effective strength of the army in the battle of Sharpsburg. From them the following statement of strength is derived:

Mansfield's command. In the mean time General Mansfield had been killed, and a portion of his corps (formerly Banks's) had also been thrown into confusion."—General Sumner's testimony, "Report on the Conduct of the War," Part I., p. 368.

[1] General Sumner's testimony, "Report on the Conduct of the War," Part I., p. 368.

The command of General Jackson embraced the division under General J. R. Jones and that under General Lawton. After General Lawton was wounded, the command of the latter division devolved upon General Early. General J. R. Jones reports the effective strength of his division to have been sixteen hundred[1] when the battle began. General Early reports the effective strength of his division as follows: Lawton's brigade, eleven hundred and fifty; Hays's brigade, five hundred and fifty; Walker's brigade, seven hundred; and his own brigade, one thousand: total effective of the division, thirty-four hundred;[2] and the total effective of Jackson's command was, therefore, five thousand men.

The command of General Longstreet, at that time, embraced the six brigades under General D. R. Jones, the two brigades under General Hood, and an unattached brigade under General N. G. Evans. His other three brigades were temporarily detached, under General R. H. Anderson.

General Jones reports his strength to have been twenty-four hundred and thirty effective.[3] The strength of Hood's division at the commencement of the campaign was thirty-eight hundred and fifty-two;[4] General Hood puts the losses of his division in its encounters with the enemy *previous* to the battle of Sharpsburg at fifteen hundred and twenty;[5] this, making no deduction for straggling, would make his effective in that engagement but twenty-three hundred and thirty-two. General Evans states that his brigade numbered twenty-two hundred effective at the opening of the campaign,[6] and reports his loss in the battles about Manassas at six hundred and thirty-one;[7] his brigade was also engaged at South Mountain, and could not have exceeded fifteen hundred

[1] "Reports of the Operations of the Army of Northern Virginia," p. 222.
[2] Ibid., pp. 190–196.   [3] Ibid., p. 219.
[4] "Return of the Army of Northern Virginia of the 20th of July, 1862," chapter xiv.
[5] "Reports of the Operations of the Army of Northern Virginia," p. 214.
[6] Ibid., p. 290.   [7] Ibid., p. 288.

effective at Sharpsburg.   General Longstreet's command, therefore, numbered six thousand two hundred and sixty-two effective. General D. H. Hill in his report puts his effective at three thousand [1] on the morning of the 17th.   General R. H. Anderson's division, embracing on this occasion the brigades of Mahone, Wright, Armistead, Wilcox, Pryor, and Featherston, and temporarily assigned to General D. H. Hill, is stated by the latter to have been three or four thousand strong; [2] call it thirty-five hundred.

General A. P. Hill's command consisted of the brigades of Branch, Gregg, Archer, Pender, and Brockenborough. He states the strength of the first three at two thousand; [3] and allowing the average of seven hundred each for the other two, we have for his division a total effective of thirty-four hundred.   The other brigade of this division (Thomas's) was left at Harper's Ferry.

The division of General McLaws consisted of the brigades of Kershaw, Barksdale, Semmes, and Cobb.   He reports the effective strength of the four brigades to have been twenty-eight hundred and ninety-three. [4]

There remains but the small division of two brigades under General J. G. Walker; General Ransom states his effective strength at sixteen hundred [5]; General Walker does not give the strength of his brigade, but I have put it at sixteen hundred, on the authority of General Ransom, who says, "So far as my memory serves me, my brigade was stronger all the time than the other of Walker's division."

With the exception of the single brigade last mentioned, the following recapitulation is established upon indisputable and contemporaneous authority, being nothing less than the testimony of the commanding officers, as shown by their official reports, made at the time:

---

[1] "Reports of the Operations of the Army of Northern Virginia," p. 114.

[2] Ibid., p. 116.   [3] Ibid., p. 129.   [4] Ibid., p. 172.   [5] Ibid., p. 291.

Longstreet's command..........................	6,262
Jackson's command....................................	5,000
D. H. Hill's division...................................	3,000
R. H. Anderson's division.............................	3,500
A. P. Hill's division..................................	3,400
McLaws's division....................................	2,893
J. G. Walker's division...............................	3,200
Total effective infantry...........................	27,255

I cannot verify the estimate made for the cavalry and artillery, viz., eight thousand; but I am sure it is rather excessive than the reverse.

This would make General Lee's entire strength thirty-five thousand two hundred and fifty-five.

General McClellan, in his official report, states that he had in action, in the same engagement, eighty-seven thousand one hundred and sixty-four of all arms.[1]

Those thirty-five thousand Confederates were the very flower of the Army of Northern Virginia, who, with indomitable courage and inflexible tenacity, wrestled for the mastery, in the ratio of one to three of their adversaries; and with consummate skill were they manœuvred and shifted from point to point, as different parts of the line of battle were in turn assailed with greatest impetuosity. The right was called upon to go to the rescue of the left; the centre was reduced to a mere shell in responding to the demands for assistance from the right and left; and A. P. Hill's command, the last to arrive from Harper's Ferry, reached the field just in time to restore the wavering right. At times it appeared as if disaster was inevitable, but succor never failed, and night found Lee's lines unbroken and his army still defiant.

The weapon used was admirably tempered; but much as we may praise the blade, we should not forget the extraordinary skill and vigor with which it was wielded in that memorable engagement by the great Confederate leader.

[1] Extract from General McClellan's "Report," "The American Conflict," p. 209.

The army of General McClellan had been too severely handled and was too badly broken to justify a renewal of the attack. In his testimony before the Committee on the Conduct of the War, that officer said ("Report," Part I., p. 441): "The next morning (the 18th) I found that our loss had been so great, and there was so much disorganization in some of the commands, that I did not consider it proper to renew the attack that day, especially as I was sure of the arrival that day of two fresh divisions, amounting to about fifteen thousand men. As an instance of the condition of some of the troops that morning, I happen to recollect the returns of the First Corps—General Hooker's—made the morning of the 18th, by which there were about thirty-five hundred men reported present for duty. Four days after that, the returns of the same corps showed thirteen thousand five hundred. I had arranged, however, to renew the attack at daybreak on the 19th."

The 18th of September, the day after the battle, passed therefore without any serious engagement. General Lee's army, as may be inferred, was in no condition to take the offensive—and on the night of that day it recrossed the Potomac River into Virginia. A force sent by General McClellan to harass the Confederate rear-guard under General A. P. Hill, who had but two thousand muskets, had the temerity to cross the Potomac in pursuit. Hill promptly made his disposition for battle, and in an incredibly short time the attacking force of the enemy was wellnigh annihilated; such as were not killed, captured, or drowned in the river in their efforts to escape, reached the Maryland side in an utterly disorganized and demoralized condition.[1]

After these events, General Lee for some time recruited

---

[1] " A simultaneous, daring charge was made, and the enemy driven pell-mell into the river. Then commenced the most terrible slaughter that this war has yet witnessed. The broad surface of the Potomac was blue with the floating bodies of our foe. But few escaped to tell the tale. By their own account, they lost three thousand men killed and drowned from one brigade alone. Some two hundred prisoners were taken."—A. P. Hill's "Report."

his army in the lower Valley of Virginia without molestation.

STRENGTH OF THE TWO ARMIES AFTER THE BATTLE.

The official return of the Army of Northern Virginia, of
the 22d of September, 1862, after our return to Virginia and
when the stragglers left behind in the extraordinary marches
in Maryland had rejoined their commands, shows present for
duty thirty-six thousand one hundred and eighty-seven infantry and artillery; the cavalry, of which there is no report,
would perhaps increase these figures to forty thousand of all
arms.

The return of the Army of the Potomac, of the 20th of
September, 1862, shows present for duty, at that date, of the
commands that participated in the battle of Sharpsburg,
eighty-five thousand nine hundred and thirty of all arms, as
follows : [1]

General McClellan, staff, engineer brigade, etc....	1,393
First Army-Corps, General Meade............	12,237
Second Army-Corps, General Sumner...............	13,604
Fifth Army-Corps, General Porter.................	19,477
Sixth Army-Corps, General Franklin.............	11,862
Ninth Army-Corps, General Burnside...............	10,734
Twelfth Army-Corps, General Williams.............	8,383
Cavalry corps, General Pleasanton...............	4,543
Detached commands at Frederick, Williamsport, and Boones-
boro..	3,697
	85,930

This is exclusive of Crouch's division of the Fourth
Corps (seven thousand two hundred and nineteen), which
reached General McClellan after the battle. The Federal
loss at Boonesboro and Antietam—or Sharpsburg—was fourteen thousand seven hundred and ninety-four.[2]

[1] *See* official return from the Adjutant-General's office, United States Army,
"Report on the Conduct of the War," Part I., p. 492.

[2] Ibid., p. 42.

Tidings reached General Lee, soon after his return to Virginia, of the serious illness of one of his daughters—the darling of his flock. For several days apprehensions were entertained that the next intelligence would be of her death. One morning the mail was received, and the private letters were distributed as was the custom; but no one knew whether any home news had been received by the general. At the usual hour he summoned me to his presence to know if there were any matters of army routine upon which his judgment and action were desired. The papers containing a few such cases were presented to him; he reviewed and gave his orders in regard to them. I then left him, but for some cause returned in a few moments, and with my accustomed freedom entered his tent without announcement or ceremony, when I was startled and shocked to see him overcome with grief, an open letter in his hands. That letter contained the sad intelligence of his daughter's death.

The reader will probably ask why this incident is introduced here.

Although apparently without special significance, it illustrates one of the noblest traits of the character of that noble man. He was the father of a tenderly-loved daughter, one who appealed with peculiar force to his paternal affection and care, and whose sweet presence he was to know no more in this world; but he was also charged with the command of an important and active army, to whose keeping to a great extent were intrusted the safety and honor of the Southern Confederacy. Lee the man must give way to Lee the patriot and soldier. His army demanded his first thought and care; to his men, to their needs, he must first attend, and then he could surrender himself to his private, personal affairs. Who can tell with what anguish of soul he endeavored to control himself, and to maintain a calm exterior, and who can estimate the immense effort necessary to still the heart filled to overflowing with tenderest emotions, and to give attention to the important trusts committed to him, before permitting the more selfish indulgence of private meditation, grief, and prayer? Duty first, was the rule of his life, and his every thought, word, and action, was made to square with duty's inexorable demands.

Scarcely less to be admired than his sublime devotion to duty was his remarkable self-control. General Lee was naturally of a positive temperament, and of strong passions; and it is a mistake to suppose him otherwise; but he held these in complete subjection to his will and conscience. He was not one of those invariably amiable men whose temper is never ruffled; but when we consider the immense burden which rested upon him, and the numberless causes for annoyance with which he had to contend, the occasional cropping-out of temper which we, who were constantly near him, witnessed, only showed how great was his habitual self-command.

He had a great dislike to reviewing army communications: this was so thoroughly appreciated by me that I would never present a paper for his action, unless it was of decided importance, and of a nature to demand his judgment and decision. On one occasion when an audience had not been asked of him for several days, it became necessary to have one. The few papers requiring his action were submitted. He was not in a very pleasant mood; something irritated him, and he manifested his ill-humor by a little nervous twist or jerk of the neck and head, peculiar to himself, accompanied by some harshness of manner. This was perceived by me, and I hastily concluded that my efforts to save him annoyance were not appreciated. In disposing of some case of a vexatious character, matters reached a climax; he became really worried, and, forgetting what was due to my superior, I petulantly threw the paper down at my side and gave evident signs of anger. Then, in a perfectly calm and measured tone of voice, he said, "Colonel Taylor, when I lose my temper, don't you let it make you angry."

Was there ever a more gentle and considerate and yet so

positive a reproof? How magnanimous in the great soldier, and yet how crushing to the subordinate! The rash and disrespectful conduct of the latter would have justified, if it did not demand, summary treatment at the hands of the former. Instead of this, the first man of his day and generation, great and glorious in his humility, condescended to occupy the same plane with his youthful subaltern, and to reason with him as an equal, frankly acknowledging his own imperfections, but kindly reminding the inferior at the same time of his duty and his position.

CHAPTER VII.

Battle of Fredericksburg.—Federal Army One Hundred Thousand strong: Confederate Army Seventy-eight Thousand strong.—Battle of Chancellorsville. —Federal Army One Hundred and Thirty-two Thousand strong: Confederate Army Fifty-seven Thousand strong.

In the latter part of October, 1862, General McClellan moved his army to the south side of the Potomac, east of the mountains. On the 4th of November he occupied Ashby's Gap. His entire army was now concentrated in the neighborhood of Warrenton. He was at this time again relieved of the command of the Army of the Potomac, and General Burnside was appointed to succeed him. After a conference with General-in-chief Halleck, the new commander determined by a rapid movement to secure possession of Fredericksburg, from which point as a base he proposed to renew the advance upon the Confederate capital. General Lee, whose army at the commencement of these movements was concentrated in the lower Valley of Virginia, had not been meanwhile inactive. Closely scrutinizing every movement of the enemy, he seemed, by intuition, to divine his purpose, and promptly made such disposition as was necessary to forestall him.

When General Burnside's intention to move upon Fredericksburg was fully developed, General Lee ordered Longstreet to that point, and directed Jackson, who was still in the Valley, to move rapidly on Orange Court-House.

Sumner's grand division led the van of the Federal army, and its advance arrived opposite Fredericksburg on the after-

noon of the 17th of November. No serious effort was made
by General Sumner to cross the river and occupy the town,
and time was thus afforded for the advance divisions of the
Confederates to reach the point threatened; so that when the
Federal commander arrived opposite, doubtless to his surprise he found no despicable array of Confederate bayonets
prepared to dispute his passage of the river. With his entire
army he soon occupied Stafford Heights; and, casting his
eye southward beyond the level plain or belt which skirts
the south bank of the river, he saw the Army of Northern
Virginia strongly posted upon the range of hills overlooking
the intervening plain. Again General Lee gave " check ! "

The nature of the ground rendered it an easy matter for
the Federal commander to control the southern bank of the
river. On the 11th of December he threw a force across,
and occupied the town. The entire army, with the exception of one corps, under General Hooker, followed, and by
the evening of the 12th was well established on the south
side.[1] As the fog lifted on the morning of the 13th, the
Confederates beheld the Army of the Potomac drawn up in
most imposing array, fully one hundred thousand strong,[2]
stretching from above Fredericksburg to Deep Run. It was
a grand and beautiful sight; rarely is one more glorious
vouchsafed to mortal eye. And now, as the command is
given to the Federal troops to advance, a new interest, a
spirit of intense excitement, is added to the scene; and as
the whole line of blue—solid and regular, bristling with the
glittering bayonets—moves steadily forward, accompanied by
the deafening roar of the artillery, the eye taking in the
whole panorama at a glance, men hold their breath, and
realize that war is indeed as glorious as it is terrible.

---

[1] Three divisions of Hooker's corps followed on the 13th, and are included
in the estimate of the Federal strength.

[2] General Burnside testified before the Committee on the Conduct of the
War that he had a hundred thousand men on the south side of the river, and in
action.—" Report on the Conduct of the War," Part I., p. 656.

The Federal soldiers advanced right gallantly to the desperate work assigned them; time and again was the assault renewed on the right and on the left of the Confederate line, but all in vain. The cool, steady veterans of Lee, under the protection of their hastily-constructed or extemporized works, made terrible havoc in the ranks of the assailing columns; and division after division recoiled from the terrible shock, shattered, discomfited, and demoralized. Their allotted task exceeded human endeavor; and no shame to them that, after such courageous and brilliant conduct, their efforts lacked success. Less than twenty thousand Confederate troops (about one-fourth of the army under General Lee)[1] were actively engaged. It was certainly the most easily won of all the grand battles of the war, and it was, indeed, the most exhilarating and inspiring to look upon, as beheld from the summit of one of the hills occupied by our troops, where army headquarters were temporarily established.

Contrary to the expectation of General Lee, the assault was not renewed,[2] and, on the night of the 15th, General Burnside retired his army from the south side of the river, and resumed his former position on Stafford Heights.

Much has been said and written about a proposition having been made to General Lee by General Jackson, that he be allowed to make a night-attack on the enemy after his repulse. Some of the features of this alleged proposition, as published some years ago, are so absurd as to carry in them-

---

[1] The returns of the Army of Northern Virginia show that on the 10th December, 1862, General Lee had present for duty seventy-eight thousand two hundred and twenty-eight, and, on the 20th December, seventy-five thousand five hundred and twenty-four of all arms, including the reserve artillery, parked some distance in the rear.

[2] "The attack on the 13th had been so easily repulsed, and by so small a part of our army, that it was not supposed the enemy would limit his efforts to one attempt, which, in view of the magnitude of his preparations and the extent of his force, seemed to be comparatively insignificant. Believing, therefore, that he would attack us, it was not deemed expedient to lose the advantages of our position, and expose the troops to the fire of his inaccessible batteries beyond the river, by advancing against him."—General Lee's "Report."

selves evidence of their fictitious character. I can only say
that I never heard of any such proposition, and I have excellent authority for asserting, as I do, that none such was ever
made.

In speaking of the engagement, General Jackson has the
following in his official report : " Repulsed on the right, left,
and centre, the enemy soon after reformed his lines, and
gave some indications of a purpose to renew the attack. I
waited some time to receive it ; but he making no forward
movement, I determined, if prudent, to do so myself. The
artillery of the enemy was so judiciously posted as to make
an advance of our troops across the plain very hazardous ; yet
it was so promising of good results, if successfully executed,
as to induce me to make preparations for the attempt. In
order to guard against disaster, the infantry was to be preceded by artillery, and the movement postponed until late in
the evening, so that, if compelled to retire, it would be under
the cover of night. Owing to unexpected delay, the movement could not be gotten ready until late in the evening.
The first gun had hardly moved forward from the wood a
hundred yards, when the enemy's artillery reopened, and so
completely swept our front as to satisfy me that the proposed
movement should be abandoned." In this, perhaps, is to be
found the explanation of, and all of truth there is in, the
report referred to.

For several months after this the army rested in winter-
quarters, and nothing of special interest occurred, save an
abortive attempt made in the midst of winter by General
Burnside to cross the river at United States Ford, in which
attempt he was completely foiled by the execrable condition
of the roads, and his troops, after floundering in the mud for
several days, returned to their camps.

The Confederate artillery, or a large portion thereof,
which was parked in the rear, near the railroad, for greater
convenience in supplying the animals with food, was ordered
forward by General Jackson—General Lee being in Rich-

mond at the time—as soon as intimation of the purpose of General Burnside was disclosed, and was much damaged in its hasty but (as events proved) unnecessary efforts to get to the front. General Burnside was compelled to relinquish whatever design he had entertained, and quiet was again established in the two opposing armies.

Active operations were resumed in the spring. General Hooker, whose turn it now was, under Federal dispensation, to wrestle with General Lee, crossed the Rappahannock in the latter part of April, 1863 ; took position at Chancellorsville, and constructed a formidable line of earthworks, from which secure position he proposed to move on General Lee's flank.

Of all the battles fought by the Army of Northern Virginia, that of Chancellorsville stands first, as illustrating the consummate audacity and military skill of commanders, and the valor and determination of the men. General Lee, with fifty-seven thousand troops of all arms, intrenched along the line of hills south of the Rappahannock, near Fredericksburg, was confronted by General Hooker, with the Army of the Potomac, one hundred and thirty-two thousand strong, occupying the bluffs on the opposite side of the river.

On the 29th of April the Federal commander essayed to put into execution an admirably-conceived plan of operations, from which he doubtless concluded that he could compel either the evacuation by General Lee of his strongly-fortified position, or else his utter discomfiture when unexpectedly and vigorously assailed upon his left flank and rear by the " finest army on the planet "—really more than twice the size of his own.

A formidable force, under General Sedgwick, was thrown across the river below Fredericksburg, and made demonstrations of an intention to assail the Confederate front. Meanwhile, with great celerity and secrecy, General Hooker, with the bulk of his army, crossed at the upper fords, and, in an able manner and wonderfully short time, had concentrated

four of his seven army-corps,[1] numbering fifty-six thousand
men, at Chancellorsville, about ten miles west of Fredericksburg. His purpose was now fully developed to General Lee
who, instead of awaiting its further prosecution, immediately
determined on the movement the least expected by his oppo-,
nent. He neither proceeded to make strong his left against
attack from the direction of Chancellorsville, nor did he
move southward, so as to put his army between that of General Hooker and the Confederate capital; but, leaving General Early, with about nine thousand men, to take care of
General Sedgwick, he moved with the remainder of his
army, numbering forty-eight thousand men, toward Chancellorsville. As soon as the advance of the enemy was encountered, it was attacked with vigor, and very soon the Federal
army was on the defensive in its apparently impregnable
position. It was not the part of wisdom to attempt to storm
this stronghold; but Sedgwick would certainly soon be at
work in the rear, and Early, with his inadequate force, could
not do more than delay and harass him. It was, therefore,
imperatively necessary to strike—to strike boldly, effectively,
and at once. There could be no delay. Meanwhile two
more army-corps had joined General Hooker, who now had
about Chancellorsville ninety-one thousand men—six corps,
except one division of the Second Corps (Couch's), which had
been left with Sedgwick, at Fredericksburg. It was a critical position for the Confederate commander, but his confidence in his trusted lieutenant and brave men was such that
he did not long hesitate. Encouraged by the counsel and
confidence of General Jackson, he determined still further
to divide his army; and while he, with the divisions of Anderson and McLaws, less than fourteen thousand men,
should hold the enemy in his front, he would hurl Jackson
upon his flank and rear, and crush and crumble him as between the upper and nether millstone. The very boldness
of the movement contributed much to insure its success.

[1] Except one division.

This battle illustrates most admirably the peculiar talent and individual excellence of Lee and Jackson. For quickness of perception, boldness in planning, and skill in directing, General Lee had no superior: for celerity in his movements, audacity in the execution of bold designs and impetuosity in attacking, General Jackson had not his peer.

The flank movement of Jackson's wing was attended with extraordinary success. On the afternoon of the 2d of May he struck such a blow to the enemy on their extreme right as to cause dismay and demoralizatian to their entire army; this advantage was promptly and vigorously followed up the next day, when Generals Lee and Stuart (the latter then in command of Jackson's wing) [1] joined elbows; and after most heroic and determined effort, their now united forces finally succeeded in storming and capturing the works of the enemy.

Meantime Sedgwick had forced Early out of the heights at Fredericksburg, and had advanced toward Chancellorsville, thus threatening the Confederate rear. General Lee having defeated the greater force, and driven it from its stronghold, now gathered up a few of the most available of his victorious brigades, and turned upon the lesser.

On the 3d of May Sedgwick's force was encountered in the vicinity of Salem Church, and its further progress checked by General McLaws, with the five brigades detached by General Lee for this service—including Wilcox's, which had been stationed at Banks's Ford. On the next day General Anderson was sent to reënforce McLaws with three additional brigades. Meanwhile, General Early had connected with these troops, and in the afternoon, so soon as dispositions could be made for attack, Sedgwick's lines were promptly assailed and broken—the main assault being made on the enemy's left by Early's troops. The situation was now a

---

[1] General Jackson fell mortally wounded late in the evening of the 2d; General A. P. Hill, who would have succeeded to the command of Jackson's wing, was also wounded, and General Stuart assumed the command.

critical one for the Federal lieutenant. Darkness came to his rescue, and on the night of the 4th he crossed to the north side of the river.

On the 5th General Lee concentrated for another assault on the new line taken up by General Hooker; but on the morning of the 6th it was ascertained that the enemy, in General Lee's language, "had sought safety beyond the Rappahannock," and the river flowed again between the hostile hosts.

Glorious as was the result of this battle to the Confederate arms, it was accompanied by a calamity in the contemplation of which the most brilliant victory of that incomparable army must ever be regarded as a supreme disaster. The star of Confederate destiny reached its zenith on the 2d day of May, when Jackson fell wounded at the head of his victorious troops; it began to set on the 10th of May, when Jackson was no more.

STRENGTH OF THE OPPOSING ARMIES.

In confirmation of the figures just given as representing the strength of the two armies, I submit the following: General Longstreet with a portion of his corps was at this time operating on the south side of James River, in the neighborhood of Suffolk. Of his command there remained with General Lee but the two divisions of Generals McLaws and Anderson. The official return of the Army of Northern Virginia, of March 31, 1863, after a long period of rest and recruiting, and when perhaps the several commands attained their greatest strength, shows, as present for duty:

Anderson's and McLaws's divisions......................... 15,649
Jackson's command....................................... 33,333
Cavalry... 6,509
Reserve artillery (parked in rear)........................ 1,621

Total of all arms...................................... 57,112

I exclude the troops serving in the Valley district—thirty-one hundred and eighty-six—included in the departmental return, but not available at Fredericksburg. This return is the nearest to the date of the battle of Chancellorsville of all those in the archive-office at Washington, and of all now in existence known to me.[1] General Early had with him at Fredericksburg his own division, and one brigade of another —in all, according to his statement, nine thousand men. General Lee remained in front of General Hooker at Chancellorsville with fourteen thousand men, viz., the two divisions of McLaws and Anderson, with the exception of Barksdale's brigade left with General Early; this estimate includes Wilcox's brigade at Banks's Ford. General Jackson had with him in his flanking movement his command, less Early's division, in round numbers say twenty-six thousand men. General Stuart had six thousand five hundred and nine sabres with which to oppose the cavalry column of the Federals, numbering twelve thousand men.

In regard to the Federal strength, I have adopted the figures given in the book of Mr. Swinton, confirmed by the evidence given before the Congressional Committee on the Conduct of the War. The Army of the Potomac, under General Hooker, consisted of seven army-corps and a body of horse, numbering one hundred and thirty-two thousand[2] present for duty, as follows:

[1] On the 20th of May, 1863, two weeks after the battle, and when Pickett's and Hood's divisions had rejoined the army, the total infantry force numbered but fifty-five thousand two hundred and sixty-two effective, from which if the strength of Pickett's and Hood's divisions is deducted, there would remain forty-one thousand three hundred and fifty-eight as the strength of the commands that participated in the battle of Chancellorsville, on the 20th of May.—*See* "Return" of the 20th of May, 1863, chapter xiv.

[2] "It" (the Army of the Potomac) "numbered one hundred and twenty thousand men, infantry and artillery, with a body of twelve thousand well-equipped cavalry, and a powerful artillery force of above four hundred guns."—Swinton's "Army of the Potomac," p. 269. In a foot-note Mr. Swinton thus substantiates his estimate of the infantry and artillery: "This estimate is approximate; the data are as follows: the effective of the Fifth, Eleventh, and Twelfth Corps was

The Fifth, Eleventh, and Twelfth Army-Corps..............	44,661
The Sixth Army-Corps.................................	22,000
The First and Third Army-Corps......................	35,000
The Second Army-Corps...............................	18,000
Total infantry and artillery......................	119,661
And the corps of cavalry.........................	12,000
Total of all arms................................	131,661

General Sedgwick's force at Falmouth and Fredericksburg originally consisted of the First, Third, and Sixth Army-Corps, and one division of the Second Corps, and numbered sixty-three thousand men, though only a portion crossed the river; it was subsequently reduced to twenty-eight thousand by the withdrawal of the First and Third Corps, which joined General Hooker. The latter, when he first moved to Chancellorsville, had with him the Fifth, Eleventh, Twelfth, and Second Corps (save one division with Sedgwick), numbering, according to the returns, fifty-six thousand men; and when he was subsequently joined by the First and Third Corps—thirty-five thousand strong (that is, previous to the assault by General Lee at Chancellorsville)—he must have had with him nearly ninety thousand men. It has already been shown that in the assault General Lee had but forty thousand men.

In this comparative statement of strength I have followed the official returns as to both armies. It is proper to state that General Hooker in his testimony before the Committee on the Conduct of the War (second series, vol. i., p. 120) puts the effective strength of the Fifth, Eleventh, and Twelfth Corps, at Chancellorsville, at thirty-six thousand

put by General Hooker, just before Chancellorsville, at forty-four thousand six hundred and sixty-one ('Report on the Conduct of the War,' second series, vol. i., p. 120). The effective of the Sixth Corps is given by General Sedgwick (ibid., p. 95) as twenty-two thousand; and the effective of the First and Third Corps, by the same authority, was thirty-five thousand. There remains the Second Corps, to which if we give a minimum of eighteen thousand, there will result the aggregate of one hundred and nineteen thousand six hundred and sixty-one."

men. He explains the discrepancy between this and the strength of these corps on the 30th of April, viz., forty-four thousand six hundred and sixty-one, by stating that the returns included the artillery, and that the greater portion of the latter did not march with the corps; he also excludes heavy detachments left with the trains, "as well as regiments left behind for discharge" (from service?). Now, the same necessity existed for General Lee to guard his trains; and, of his strength, quite as large a proportion of the artillery was not up. None of the reserve artillery which I have included in my estimate of the Confederate strength was engaged, being some miles in rear at the time. But even adopting General Hooker's estimate of the three corps mentioned, then adding twelve thousand for that portion of the Second which joined him (all but Gibbon's division), and the First and Third Corps—thirty-five thousand, as given by General Sedgwick—and his strength at Chancellorsville, exclusive of Pleasanton's cavalry, was eighty-three thousand. The testimony of General Hancock and General Sedgwick confirms this estimate.

CHAPTER VIII.

The Pennsylvania Campaign.—The Battle of Gettysburg.—Strength of the Opposing Armies.

From the very necessities of the case, the general theory upon which the war was conducted on the part of the South was one of defense. The great superiority of the North in men and material made it indispensable for the South to husband its resources as much as possible, inasmuch as the hope of ultimate success which the latter entertained, rested rather upon the dissatisfaction and pecuniary distress which a prolonged war would entail upon the former—making the people weary of the struggle—than upon any expectation of conquering a peace by actually subduing so powerful an adversary.

Nevertheless, in the judgment of General Lee, it was a part of a true defensive policy to take the aggressive when good opportunity offered; and by delivering an effective blow to the enemy, not only to inflict upon him serious loss, but at the same time to thwart his designs of invasion, derange the plan of campaign contemplated by him, and thus prolong the conflict.

The Federal army, under General Hooker, had now reoccupied the heights opposite Fredericksburg, where it could not be attacked except at a disadvantage. Instead of quietly awaiting the pleasure of the Federal commander in designing and putting into execution some new plan of campaign, General Lee determined to manœuvre to draw him from his impregnable position and if possible to remove the scene of hostilities beyond the Potomac. His design was to free the State of Virginia, for a time at least, from the presence of the enemy, to transfer the theatre of war to Northern soil, and, by selecting a favorable time and place in which to receive the attack which his adversary would be compelled to make on him, to take the reasonable chances of defeating him in a pitched battle; knowing full well that to obtain such an advantage there would place him in position to attain far more decisive results than could be hoped for from a like advantage gained in Virginia. But even if unable to attain the valuable results which might be expected to follow a decided advantage gained over the enemy in Maryland or Pennsylvania, it was thought that the movement would at least so far disturb the Federal plan for the summer campaign as to prevent its execution during the season for active operations.[1]

In pursuance of this design, early in the month of June, General Lee moved his army northward by way of Culpeper, and thence to and down the Valley of Virginia to Winchester.

The army had now been reorganized into three armycorps, designated the First, Second, and Third Corps, and commanded respectively by Lieutenant-Generals Longstreet, Ewell, and A. P. Hill.

The Second Corps was in advance, and crossed the branches of the Shenandoah, near Front Royal, on the 12th of June. Brushing aside the force of the enemy under General Milroy, that occupied the lower Valley—most of which was captured and the remnant of which sought refuge in the fortifications at Harper's Ferry[2]—General Ewell crossed the

[1] General Lee's "Report."

[2] "These operations resulted in the expulsion of the enemy from the Valley, the capture of four thousand prisoners, with a corresponding number of small-arms, twenty-eight pieces of superior artillery, including those taken by General Rodes and General Hays, about three hundred wagons and as many horses, together with a considerable quantity of ordnance, commissary, and quartermaster's stores."—General Lee's "Report of the Pennsylvania Campaign."

'Potomac River with his three divisions in the latter part of June, and, in pursuance of the orders of General Lee, traversed Maryland and advanced into Pennsylvania.

General A. P. Hill, whose corps was the last to leave the line of the Rappahannock, followed with his three divisions in Ewell's rear. General Longstreet covered these movements with his corps; then moved by Ashby's and Snicker's Gaps into the Valley and likewise crossed the Potomac River, leaving to General Stuart the task of holding the gaps of the Blue Ridge Mountains with his corps of cavalry.

The Federal commander had meanwhile moved his army so as to cover Washington City; and, as soon as he was thoroughly informed, by Ewell's rapid advance, of the real intention of his adversary, he too crossed into Maryland.

On the 27th of June General Lee was near Chambersburg with the First and Third Corps, the Second being still in advance, but within supporting distance.

With the exception of the cavalry, the army was well in hand. The absence of that indispensable arm of the service was most seriously felt by General Lee. He had directed General Stuart to use his discretion as to where and when to cross the river—that is, he was to cross east of the mountains, or retire through the mountain-passes into the Valley and cross in the immediate rear of the infantry, as the movements of the enemy and his own judgment should determine—but he was expected to maintain communication with the main column, and especially directed to keep the commanding general informed of the movements of the Federal army.

The army continued to advance. On the 1st of July General Lee reached Cashtown and stopped to confer with General A. P. Hill, whose corps was concentrating at that point, and who reported that the advance of Heth's division had encountered the cavalry of the enemy near Gettysburg. Instructions had been sent to General Heth to ascertain what force was at Gettysburg, and, if he found infantry opposed to him, to report the fact immediately, without forcing an engagement.

No tidings whatever had been received from or of our cavalry under General Stuart since crossing the river; and General Lee was consequently without accurate information of the movements or position of the main Federal army.[1] An army without cavalry in a strange and hostile country is as a man deprived of his eyesight and beset by enemies; he may be never so brave and strong, but he cannot intelligently administer a single effective blow.

The sound of artillery was soon heard in the direction of Gettysburg. General Hill hastened to the front. General Lee followed.

On arriving at the scene of battle, General Lee ascertained that the enemy's infantry and artillery were present in considerable force. Heth's division was already hotly engaged, and it was soon evident that a serious engagement could not be avoided.

Orders had previously been sent to General Ewell to recall his advanced divisions, and to concentrate about Cashtown. While *en route* for that point, on the morning of the 1st of July, General Ewell learned that Hill's corps was moving toward Gettysburg, and, on arriving at Middletown, he

---

[1] "On the morning of the 29th of June the Third Corps, composed of the divisions of Major-Generals Anderson, Heth, and Pender, and five battalions of artillery, under command of Colonel R. L. Walker, was encamped on the road from Chambersburg to Gettysburg, near the village of Fayetteville. I was directed to move on this road in the direction of York, and to cross the Susquehanna, menacing the communications of Harrisburg with Philadelphia, and to coöperate with General Ewell, acting as circumstances might require. Accordingly, on the 29th I moved General Heth's division to Cashtown, some eight miles from Gettysburg, following on the morning of the 30th with the division of General Pender, and directing General Anderson to move in the same direction on the morning of the 1st of July. On arriving at Cashtown General Heth, who had sent forward Pettigrew's brigade to Gettysburg, reported that Pettigrew had encountered the enemy at Gettysburg, principally cavalry, but in what force he could not determine. A courier was then dispatched with this information to the general commanding."—Extract from A. P. Hill's "Report," "Southern Historical Society Papers," November, 1876.

turned the head of his column in that direction. When within a few miles of the town, General Rodes, whose division was in advance, was made aware, by the sharp cannonading, of the presence of the enemy in force at Gettysburg, and caused immediate preparations for battle to be made.

On reaching the scene of conflict, General Rodes made his dispositions to assail the force with which Hill's troops were engaged, but no sooner were his lines formed than he perceived fresh troops of the enemy extending their right flank, and deploying in his immediate front. With this force he was soon actively engaged. The contest now became sharp and earnest. Neither side sought or expected a general engagement; and yet, brought thus unexpectedly in the presence of each other, found a conflict unavoidable.

The battle continued, with varying success, until perhaps 3 P. M., when General Early, of Ewell's corps, reached the field with his division, moved in on Rodes's left, and attacked the enemy with his accustomed vigor and impetuosity. This decided the contest. The enemy's right gave way under Early's assault. Pender's division, of Hill's corps, had meanwhile been advanced to relieve that of Heth; and Rodes, observing the effect of Early's attack, ordered his line forward. There resulted a general and irresistible advance of our entire line; the enemy gave way at all points, and were driven in disorder through and beyond the town of Gettysburg, leaving over five thousand prisoners in our hands.

In this action the force engaged on the Confederate side, as already stated, consisted of the divisions of Heth and Pender, of Hill's corps, and those of Early and Rodes, of Ewell's corps. On the side of the Federals there was the First Corps, embracing the divisions of Wadsworth, Doubleday, and Robinson; the Eleventh Corps, embracing the divisions of Schurz, Barlow, and Steinwehr; and the cavalry force under General Buford. The infantry force on each side was about the same,[1] and the preponderance in numbers was with

[1] The four divisions of Confederates had an average strength of six thousand

the Federals, to the extent of General Buford's cavalry command.

General Lee witnessed the flight of the Federals through Gettysburg and up the hills beyond. He then directed me to go to General Ewell and to say to him that, from the position which he occupied, he could see the enemy retreating over those hills, without organization and in great confusion, that it was only necessary to press " those people " in order to secure possession of the heights, and that, if possible, he wished him to do this. In obedience to these instructions, I proceeded immediately to General Ewell and delivered the order of General Lee ; and, after receiving from him some message for the commanding general in regard to the prisoners captured, returned to the latter and reported that his order had been delivered.

General Ewell did not express any objection, or indicate the existence of any impediment, to the execution of the order conveyed to him, but left the impression upon my mind that it would be executed. In the exercise of that discretion, however, which General Lee was accustomed to accord to his lieutenants, and probably because of an undue regard for his admonition, given early in the day, not to precipitate a general engagement, General Ewell deemed it unwise to make the pursuit. The troops were not moved forward, and the enemy proceeded to occupy and fortify the po-

when General Lee started on this campaign, reduced at this date to about five thousand five hundred, as will be shown later in this narrative ; making the total engaged in the action of the first day twenty-two thousand. It could not have exceeded twenty-four thousand. General Butterfield, chief of staff of the Army of the Potomac, testified before the Committee on the Conduct of the War ("Report," second series, p. 428) that on the 10th of June the First Corps had eleven thousand three hundred and fifty, and the Eleventh Corps ten thousand one hundred and seventy-seven, present for duty ; and that previous to the battle of Gettysburg the First Corps was increased by the addition of Stannard's Vermont Brigade. It would appear, then, that the First and Eleventh Corps, at the time of the engagement, had a total strength of from twenty-two to twenty-four thousand. Mr. Swinton puts the loss sustained by these two corps at "near ten thousand men."

sition which it was designed that General Ewell should seize.

Major-General Edward Johnson, whose division reached the field after the engagement, and formed on the left of Early, in a conversation had with me, since the war, about this circumstance, in which I sought an explanation of our inaction at that time, assured me that there was no hinderance to his moving forward; but that, after getting his command in line of battle, and before it became seriously engaged or had advanced any great distance, for some unexplained reason, he had received orders to halt. This was after General Lee's message was delivered to General Ewell.

Such was the condition of affairs when darkness veiled the scene on the evening of the first day. The prevailing idea with General Lee was, to press forward without delay; to follow up promptly and vigorously the advantage already gained. Having failed to reap the full fruit of the victory before night, his mind was evidently occupied with the idea of renewing the assault upon the enemy's right with the dawn of day on the second. The divisions of Major-Generals Early and Rodes, of Ewell's corps, had been actively engaged, and had sustained some loss, but were still in excellent condition, and in the full enjoyment of the prestige of success and a consequent elation of spirit, in having so gallantly swept the enemy from their front, through the town of Gettysburg, and compelled him to seek refuge behind the heights beyond. The division of Major-General Edward Johnson, of the same corps, was perfectly fresh, not having been engaged. Anderson's division, of Hill's corps, was also now up. With this force General Lee thought that the enemy's position could be assailed with every prospect of success; but, after a conference with the corps and division commanders on our left, who represented that, in their judgment, it would be hazardous to attempt to storm the strong position occupied by the enemy, with troops somewhat fagged by the marching and fighting of the first day;

that the ground in their immediate front furnished greater obstacles to a successful assault than existed at other points of the line, and that it could be reasonably concluded, since they had so severely handled the enemy in their front, that he would concentrate and fortify with special reference to resisting a further advance just there, he determined to make the main attack well on the enemy's left, indulging the hope that Longstreet's corps would be up in time to begin the movement at an early hour on the 2d. He instructed General Ewell to be prepared to coöperate by a simultaneous advance by his corps. General Longstreet was unexpectedly detained, however, as will best appear from the following extract from his report of the Gettysburg campaign. In speaking of his movements on the 1st *day of July,* he says :

Our march on this day was greatly delayed by Johnson's division, of the Second Corps, which came into the road from Shippensburg, and the long wagon-trains that followed him. McLaws's division, however, reached Marsh Creek, four miles from Gettysburg, a little after dark, and Hood's division got within nearly the same distance of the town about twelve o'clock at night. Law's brigade was ordered forward to its division during the day, and joined about noon on the 2d.

Previous to his joining I received instructions from the commanding general to move with the portion of my command that was up around to gain the Emmettsburg road on the enemy's left. The enemy, having been driven back by the corps of Lieutenant-Generals Ewell and A. P. Hill the day previous, had taken a strong position extending from the hill at the cemetery along the Emmettsburg road.

Fearing that my force was too weak to venture to make an attack, I delayed until General Law's brigade joined its division. As soon after his arrival as we could make our preparations, the movement was begun.

Engineers, sent out by the commanding general and myself, guided us by a road which would have completely disclosed the move. Some delay ensued in seeking a more concealed route. McLaws's division got into position opposite the enemy's left about 4 P. M. Hood's division was moved on farther to our right, and got into position, partially enveloping the enemy's left.

General Longstreet here explains the cause of the delay in bringing up his troops on the *first day;* but, notwithstanding this, the divisions of Hood and McLaws (with the exception of Law's brigade) encamped within four miles of Gettysburg at midnight of the 1st of July. He then received instructions to move *with the portion of his command that was then up,* to gain the Emmettsburg road on the enemy's left; but fearing that his force was too weak to venture to make an attack, he delayed until Law's brigade joined its division, about noon on the 2d.

In this, General Longstreet clearly admits that he assumed the responsibility of postponing the execution of the orders of the commanding general. Owing to the causes assigned, the troops were not in position to attack until 4 P. M. One can imagine what was going on in the Federal lines meanwhile. Round Top, the key to their position, which was not occupied in the morning, they now held in force, and another corps (Sedgwick's) had reached the field.

Late as it was, the original plan was adhered to. The two divisions of Longstreet's corps gallantly advanced, forced the enemy back a considerable distance, and captured some trophies and prisoners.

Ewell's divisions were ordered forward, and likewise gained additional ground and trophies.

On Cemetery Hill the attack by Early's leading brigades was made with vigor. They drove the enemy back into the works on the crest, into which they forced their way, and seized several pieces of artillery; but they were compelled to relinquish what they had gained, from want of expected support on their right, and retired to their original position, bringing with them some prisoners and four stands of colors. In explanation of this lack of expected support, General Rodes, who was on General Early's right, states in his report that after he had conferred with General Early, on his left, and General Lane, on his right, and arranged to attack in concert, he proceeded at once to make the necessary preparations; but as he had to draw his troops out of the town by the flank, change the direction of the line of battle, and then traverse a distance of twelve or fourteen hundred yards, while General Early had to move only half that distance, without change of front, it resulted that, before he drove in the enemy's skirmishers, General Early had attacked, and been compelled to withdraw.

The whole affair was disjointed. There was an utter absence of accord in the movements of the several commands, and no decisive result attended the operations of the second day.

It is generally conceded that General Longstreet, on this occasion, was fairly chargeable with tardiness, and I have always thought that his conduct, in this particular, was due to a lack of appreciation on his part of the circumstances which created an urgent and peculiar need for the presence of his troops at the front.

As soon as the necessity for the concentration of the army was precipitated by the unexpected encounter on the 1st of July with a large force of the enemy near Gettysburg, General Longstreet was urged to hasten his march, and this, perhaps, should have sufficed to cause him to push his divisions on toward Gettysburg, from which point he was distant but four miles, early on the 2d; but I cannot say that he was notified, on the night of the 1st, of the attack proposed to be made on the morning of the 2d, and the part his corps was to take therein. Neither do I think it just to charge that he was alone responsible for the delay in attacking that ensued *after* his arrival on the field. I well remember how General Lee was chafed by the non-appearance of the troops, until he finally became restless, and rode back to meet General Longstreet, and urge him forward; but, then, there was considerable delay in putting the troops to work after they reached the field, and much time was spent in discussing what was to be done, which, perhaps, could not be avoided. At any rate, it would be unreasonable to hold General Longstreet alone accountable for this.

Indeed, great injustice has been done him in the charge that he had orders from the commanding general to attack the enemy at sunrise on the 2d of July, and that he disobeyed these orders. This would imply that he was in position to attack, whereas General Lee but anticipated his early arrival on the 2d, and based his calculations upon it. I have shown how he was disappointed, and I need hardly add that the delay was fatal. In this connection, I submit the following correspondence:

NEW ORLEANS, LA., *April* 20, 1875.

MY DEAR COLONEL: Upon reading an address by Mr. Pendleton, published in the December number of the *Southern Magazine*, I saw for the first time that General Lee had ordered me to attack the left of the Federal army at "sunrise," on the second day of the battle of Gettysburg.

It occurs to me that if General Lee had any such idea as an attack at sunrise, you must surely be advised of it. Right sure am I that such an order was never delivered to me, and it is not possible for me to believe that he ever entertained an idea that I was to attack at that hour. My two divisions, nor myself, did not reach General Lee until 8 A. M. on the 2d, and if he had intended to attack at sunrise he surely would have expressed some surprise, or made some allusion to his orders.

Please do me the favor to let me know what you know of this sunrise attack. . . .

I remain very respectfully and truly yours,

JAMES LONGSTREET.

Colonel W. H. TAYLOR, *Norfolk, Virginia.*

NORFOLK, VA., *April* 28, 1875.

DEAR GENERAL: I have received your letter of the 20th inst. I have not read the article of which you speak, nor have I ever seen a copy of General Pendleton's address; indeed, I have read little or nothing of what has been written since the war: in the first place, because I could not spare the time; and, in the second, because, of those of whose writings I have heard, I deem but very few entitled to any attention whatever.

I can only say that I never before heard of the "sunrise attack" you were to have made, as charged by General Pendleton. If such an order was given you, I never knew it, or it has strangely escaped my memory. I think it more than·probable that, if General Lee had had your troops available the evening previous to the day of which you speak, he would have ordered an early attack; but this does not touch the point at issue.

I regard it as a great mistake on the part of those who, perhaps because of political differences, now undertake to criticise and attack your war record. Such conduct is most ungenerous, and I am sure meets the disapprobation of all good Confederates with whom I have the pleasure of associating in the daily walks of life.

Yours very respectfully and truly,

W. H. TAYLOR.

General JAMES LONGSTREET, New Orleans.

Since the date of this correspondence, several communications have appeared in the public prints, from the pen of General Longstreet, in reference to the battle of Gettysburg. He claims that General Lee gave battle there in spite of his remonstrances. Had such been the fact, it would work no discredit to General Lee, though at variance with his usual propensity to defer to such objections on the part of his lieutenants; but I never heard of it before, neither is it consistent with General Longstreet's assertion to Mr. Swinton, since made, that at the time in question "the Army of Northern Virginia was in condition to undertake anything." In this opinion he but expressed the sentiment of the whole army; an overweening confidence possessed us all. Now, in a retrospective view of the results attained, it is easy to conclude that it would have been well not to have attacked the third day. But did we accomplish all that could have been

reasonably expected? And if we failed to attain results
reasonably to be expected of an army in condition to undertake *anything*, how did it happen?

General Lee determined to renew the attack upon the
enemy's position on the 3d day of July. In his report of
the campaign, in speaking of the operations of the second
day, he says:

> The result of this day's operations induced the belief that,
> with proper concert of action, and with the increased support
> that the positions gained on the right would enable the artillery
> to render the assaulting columns, we should ultimately succeed;
> and it was accordingly determined to continue the attack.

> The general plan was unchanged. Longstreet, reënforced by
> Pickett's three brigades, which arrived near the battle-field dur-
> ing the afternoon of the 2d, was ordered to attack the next
> morning; and General Ewell was directed to assail the enemy's
> right at the same time.

> General Longstreet's dispositions were not completed as
> early as was expected; it appears that he was delayed by
> apprehensions that his troops would be taken in reverse as
> they advanced. General Ewell, who had orders to coöperate
> with General Longstreet, and who was, of course, not aware
> of any impediment to the main attack arranged to be made
> on the enemy's left, having reënforced General Johnson,
> whose division was upon our extreme left during the night
> of the 2d, ordered him forward early the next morning.

> In obedience to these instructions, General Johnson be-
> came hotly engaged before General Ewell could be informed
> of the halt which had been called on our right.

> After a gallant and prolonged struggle, in which the enemy
> was forced to abandon part of his intrenchments, General John-
> son found himself unable to carry the strongly-fortified crest of
> the hill. The projected attack on the enemy's left not having
> been made, he was enabled to hold his right with a force largely
> superior to that of General Johnson, and finally to threaten his

flank and rear, rendering it necessary for him to retire to his original position about 1 P. M.[1]

General Lee then had a conference with General Longstreet, and the mode of attack and the troops to make it were thoroughly debated. I was present, and understood the arrangement to be that General Longstreet should endeavor to force the enemy's lines in his front. That front was held by the divisions of Hood and McLaws. To strengthen him for the undertaking, it was decided to reënforce him by such troops as could be drawn from the centre.

Pickett's division, of Longstreet's corps, was then up, fresh and available. Heth's division, of Hill's corps, was also mentioned as available, having in great measure recuperated since its active engagement of the first day;[2] so also were the brigades of Lane and Scales, of Pender's division, Hill's corps; and as our extreme right was comparatively safe, being well posted, and not at all threatened, one of the divisions of Hood and McLaws, and the greater portion of the other, could be moved out of the lines and be made to take part in the attack. Indeed, it was designed originally that the two divisions last named, reënforced by Pickett, should make the attack; and it was only because of the apprehensions of General Longstreet that his corps was not strong enough for the movement, that General Hill was called on to reënforce him.

Orders were sent to General Hill to place Heth's division and two brigades of Pender's at General Longstreet's disposal, and to be prepared to give him further assistance if requested.

The assault was to have been made with a column of not

[1] Extract from General Lee's "Report."

[2] NOTE BY COLONEL VENABLE.—"They were terribly mistaken about Heth's division in this planning. It had not recuperated, having suffered more than was reported on the first day. Heth had suffered heavily on the 1st, before Pender and Rodes got up. He had gone almost into Gettysburg. Rodes found dead Mississippians on the wooded hill just above the town."—C. S. V.

less than two divisions, and the remaining divisions were to
have been moved forward in support of those in advance.
This was the result of the conference alluded to as understood by me.

Lieutenant-General A. P. Hill appears to have had the
same impression, for he says in his report of the operations
of his corps at this time: " I was directed to hold my line
with Anderson's division and the half of Pender's, now commanded by General Lane, and to order Heth's division, commanded by Pettigrew, and Lane's and Scales's brigades, of
Pender's division, to report to Lieutenant-General Longstreet
as a support to his corps, in the assault on the enemy's lines."

General Longstreet proceeded at once to make the dispositions for attack, and General Lee rode along the portion
of the line held by A. P. Hill's corps, and finally took position about the Confederate centre, on an elevated point, from
which he could survey the field and watch the result of the
movement.

After a heavy artillery fire along the entire line, and at
a given signal, the movement began, but the plan agreed on
was not carried out. The only troops that participated in
the attack were the divisions of Pickett (First Corps) and
Heth (Third Corps)—the latter, since the wounding of General Heth, commanded by General Pettigrew—and the brigades of Lane, Scales, and Wilcox. The two divisions were
formed in advance—the three brigades as their support.
The divisions of Hood and McLaws (First Corps) were passive spectators of the movement.

To one who observed the charge, it appeared that Pettigrew's line was not a continuation of that of Pickett, but
that it advanced in echelon. It would seem that there was
some confusion in forming the troops, for Captain Louis G.
Young, of General Pettigrew's staff, says:

On the morning of the 3d of July, General Pettigrew, commanding Heth's division, was instructed to report to General
Longstreet, who directed him to form *in the rear* of Pickett's divi-

sion, and support his advance upon Cemetery Hill, which would be commenced as soon as the fire from our artillery should have driven the enemy from his guns and prepared the way for attack. And I presume that it was in consequence of this having been the first plan settled on, that the erroneous report was circulated that Heth's division was assigned the duty of supporting that of Pickett. But the order referred to was countermanded almost as soon as given, and General Pettigrew was instructed to advance *upon the same line* with Pickett, a portion of Pender's division acting as supports.

Wilcox's brigade was ordered to support Pickett's right flank, and the brigades of Lane and Scales acted as supports to Heth's division.

General Lane, in his report, says :

General Longstreet ordered me to form in rear of the *right* of Heth's division, commanded by General Pettigrew. Soon after I had executed this order, putting Lowrance on the right, I was relieved of the command of the division by Major-General Trimble, who acted under the same orders that I had received. Heth's division was much longer than Lowrance's brigade and my own, which constituted its only support, and there was, consequently, *no second line in rear of its left.*

The assaulting column really consisted of Pickett's division—two brigades in front, and one in the second line as a support [1]—with the brigade of Wilcox in rear of its right to protect that flank; while Heth's division moved forward on Pickett's left in échelon, or with the alignment so imperfect and so drooping on the left as to appear in échelon,[2] with Lane's and Scales's brigades in rear of its right, and its left without reserve or support, and entirely exposed.

Thus the column moved forward. It is needless to say a word here of the heroic conduct of Pickett's division ; that

---

[1] Pickett had but three brigades at Gettysburg: Corse had been left with his brigade at Hanover Junction.

[2] "It was formed in échelon a hundred yards in rear."—C. S. VENABLE.

charge has already passed into history as " one of the world's great deeds of arms." While, doubtless, many brave men of other commands reached the crest of the height, this was the only organized body that entered the works of the enemy.[1] Much can be said in excuse for the failure of the other commands to fulfill the task assigned them. As a general rule, the peculiarly rough and wooded character of the country in which our army was accustomed to operate, and which in some respects was unfavorable for the manœuvres of large armies, was of decided advantage to us ; for, in moving upon the enemy through bodies of woods, or in a broken, rolling country, not only was the enemy at a loss how to estimate our strength, but our own men were not impressed with that sense of insecurity which must have resulted from a thorough knowledge of their own weakness.

[1] " The troops moved steadily on under a heavy fire of musketry and artillery, the main attack being directed against the enemy's left centre. His batteries reopened as soon as they appeared. Our own, having nearly exhausted their ammunition in the protracted cannonade that preceded the advance of the infantry, were unable to reply, or render the necessary support to the attacking party. Owing to this fact, which was unknown to me when the assault took place, the enemy was enabled to throw a strong force of infantry against our left, already wavering under a concentrated fire of artillery from the ridge in front, and from Cemetery Hill on the left. It finally gave way, and the right, after penetrating the enemy's lines, entering his advance-works, and capturing some of his artillery, was attacked simultaneously in front and on both flanks, and driven back with heavy loss."—Extract from General Lee's " Report," " Southern Historical Society Papers," July, 1876, p. 44.

In justice to the gallant men and officers of Heth's division, I here append the testimony of Captain Louis G. Young, aide to General Pettigrew, who, in describing the part taken in the third day's fight by the division, says : " Under this fire from artillery and musketry, the brigade on our left, reduced almost to a line of skirmishers, gave way. Pettigrew's and Archer's brigades advanced a little farther, and in perfect continuation of Pickett's line, which arrived at the works before we did, only because they jutted out in his front, and because his had to move over a considerably shorter distance. The right of the line, formed by Archer's and Pettigrew's brigades, rested on the works, while the left was, of course, farther removed, say forty to sixty yards. Subjected to a fire even more fatal than that which had driven back the brigade on our left, and the men listening in vain for the cheering commands of officers, who had, alas! fallen, our brigade gave way likewise, and, *simultaneously* with it, the whole line."

It was different here. The charge was made down a gentle slope, and then up to the enemy's lines, a distance of over half a mile, denuded of forests, and in full sight of the enemy, and perfect range of their artillery. These combined causes produced their natural effect upon Pettigrew's division and the brigades supporting it, caused them to falter, and finally retire. Then Pickett's division continuing the charge without supports, and in the sight of the enemy, was not half so formidable or effective as it would have been had trees or hills prevented the enemy from so correctly estimating the strength of the attacking column, and our own troops from experiencing that sense of weakness which the known absence of support necessarily produced. In spite of all this, it steadily and gallantly advanced to its allotted task. As the three brigades under Garnett, Armistead, and Kemper, approach the enemy's lines, a most terrific fire of artillery and small-arms is concentrated upon them; but they swerve not—there is no faltering; steadily moving forward, they rapidly reduce the intervening space, and close with their adversaries: leaping the breastworks, they drive back the enemy, and plant their standards on the captured guns, amid shouts of victory—dearly won and short-lived victory.

No more could be exacted, or expected, of those men of brave hearts and nerves of steel; but where are the supports to reap the benefit of their heroic efforts, and gather the fruits of a victory so nobly won? Was that but a forlorn hope, on whose success, not only in penetrating the enemy's lines, but in maintaining its hold against their combined and united efforts to dislodge it, an entire army was to wait in quiet observation? Was it designed to throw these few brigades—originally, at the most, but two divisions—upon the fortified stronghold of the enemy, while, full half a mile away, seven-ninths of the army in breathless suspense, in ardent admiration and fearful anxiety, watched, but moved not? I maintain that such was not the design of the commanding general. Had the veteran divisions of Hood and

McLaws been moved forward, as was planned, in support of
those of Pickett and Pettigrew,[1] not only would the latter
division, in all probability, have gained the enemy's works,
as did that of Pickett, but these two would have been enabled,
with the aid of Hood and McLaws, to resist all efforts of the
enemy to dislodge them.   The enemy closing in on Pickett's
brigades, concentrating upon that small band of heroes the
fire of every gun that could be brought to bear upon them,
soon disintegrated and overpowered them.   Such as were
not killed, disabled, and made captive, fell back to our lines.

It appears that General Longstreet deemed it necessary
to defend his right flank and rear with the divisions of Mc-
Laws and Hood.   These divisions, as before stated, constituted all of the Confederate line held by Longstreet's troops,
and it is not apparent how they were necessary to defend
his flank and rear.   The nearest infantry force of the enemy
to our right occupied the hills—Round Top and Little Round
Top—and the only force that could be said to have threatened our flank and rear consisted of a few brigades of cavalry, so posted as to protect the enemy's left.

It is not my purpose here to undertake to establish the
wisdom of an attack on the enemy's position on the third
day, which General Longstreet contends was opposed by his
judgment, and of which, he says, he would have stayed the
execution, had he felt that he had the privilege so to do ; nor
do I propose to discuss the necessities of his position, which
he represents to have been such as to forbid the employment
of McLaws's and Hood's divisions in the attack ; neither do I
seek any other than a just explanation of the causes of our
failure at that time; but well recalling my surprise and disappointment when it was ascertained that only Pickett's
division and the troops from Hill's corps had taken part in
the movement, and with positively distinct impressions as

---

[1] " As they were ordered to do by General Lee, for I heard him give the orders
when arranging the fight; and called his attention to it long afterward, when
there was discussion about it.   He said, 'I know it! I know it!'"—Colonel C.
S. VENABLE.

to the occurrences just related, I deem it proper to record
them for confirmation or refutation as the undisputed facts
of the case, and the testimony of others, may determine.[1]

[1] The following correspondence explains itself, and is submitted, without
comment, in connection with the assertions of fact just made:

NORFOLK, VA., *January* 29, 1877.
General JAMES LONGSTREET, *New Orleans.*

DEAR GENERAL: I have been anxious to ascertain definitely the relative
strength of the two opposing armies during the war, and, after devoting my odd
moments to an investigation of the matter for a long time past, I have at last
succeeded in reaching a satisfactory result. In putting these matters in shape,
and in order to give continuity and connection to the notes, I have touched upon
the more important incidents in General Lee's career, placing on record my
recollection of facts, and sustaining myself as much as possible by the contemporaneous testimony of those who participated in the several events.

In regard to the third day's operations at Gettysburg, according to my recollection, General Lee had a conference with you as to the attack to be made
that day, when it was determined that an assault should be made on your front,
by your corps, reënforced by Heth's division and two brigades of Pender's.
My recollection is distinct in that *all* of your divisions were to take part in the
assault, and I never did understand why Hood and McLaws were never
ordered forward. Colonel Venable agrees with me entirely in this particular.

I write, therefore, to say that if you differ from me, or care to present any
explanation of the non-action of Hood and McLaws, I should be pleased to have
any statement you may make accompany that which I propose to present in
my notes.

My desire is to do what I can toward eliminating the truth from the mass of
contradictory evidence that exists, and particularly anxious am I to avoid doing
injustice to any one, especially to one who dealt such vigorous blows for the
South, and whom I learned, during the war, to esteem so highly as yourself.
                    Yours respectfully,   W. H. TAYLOR.

                                        NEW ORLEANS, LA., *February* 2, 1877.
Colonel W. H. TAYLOR, *Norfolk, Va.*

MY DEAR SIR: I have your esteemed favor of the 29th ult., and have noted
its contents.

In reply to your inquiry for a statement in regard to the supposed orders of
General Lee in reference to the battle of the third day, I have only to say that
General Lee gave no orders for placing the divisions of McLaws and Hood in
the column of attack on that day. I cannot, therefore, have any explanation to
make at this time why these divisions were not in that column.

In putting your notes upon the events of the war together for publication, it
seems to me that care should be had that undue influences should not give
shape or tone to them. Least of all should you omit items that you may deem
essential to General Lee's vindication, upon account of kindly feelings that may
have subsisted between us. Nor do I know of good reasons why a report of
your views upon matters of public history should interrupt personal relations.

I have the privilege of giving my account afterward, and am quite willing to
have a minute investigation of Gettysburg, and to have the world know my connection with it from the inception of the campaign to its close.

I remain, very respectfully, your obedient servant,
                                        JAMES LONGSTREET.

After the assault on the enemy's works on the 3d of July, there was no serious fighting at Gettysburg. The 4th passed in comparative quiet. Neither army evinced any disposition to assail the other. Notwithstanding the brilliant achievements of Ewell and Hill on the first day, and the decided advantage gained by Longstreet on the second, the failure of the operations of the third day, involving, as they did, but two divisions of the army, deprived us of the prestige of our previous successes, and gave a shadow of right to our adversary's claim of having gained a victory. Their exultation, however, should be tempered with moderation, when we consider that, after one day of absolute quiet, the Confederates withdrew from their front without serious molestation, and with bridges swept away, and an impassable river in rear, stood in an attitude of defiance until their line of retreat could be rendered practicable, after which they safely recrossed into Virginia. Then, again, so serious was the loss visited upon the Federals in the engagements of the first and second days, and so near success was the effort to storm their position on the third day, that they were themselves undecided as to whether they should stand or retreat. In discussing several councils or conferences held by General Meade with his corps-commanders, General Sickles testified, before the Committee on the Conduct of the War, that the reason the Confederates were not followed up was on account of differences of opinion whether or not the Federals should themselves retreat, as " it was by no means clear, in the judgment of the corps-commanders, or of the general in command, whether they had won or not." [1]

EFFECTIVE STRENGTH OF THE TWO ARMIES IN THE GETTYSBURG CAMPAIGN.

It appears from the official returns on file in the War Department, that on the 31st of May, 1863, the Army of Northern Virginia numbered: infantry, fifty-four thousand

[1] " Report on the Conduct of the War," second series, vol. i., p. 302, 1865.

three hundred and fifty-six; cavalry, nine thousand five hundred and thirty-six; and artillery, four thousand four hundred and sixty; of all arms, sixty-eight thousand three hundred and fifty-two effective. This was immediately before the invasion of Pennsylvania, and may be regarded as representing the maximum of General Lee's army in the Gettysburg campaign.

At the time of that return the army was divided into but two corps or wings, one under Longstreet, and the other—Jackson's old corps—under A. P. Hill. The former embraced the divisions of McLaws, Anderson, Pickett, and Hood; and the latter those of A. P. Hill, Early, Rodes, and Johnson. Immediately after the date of this return, the army was reorganized into three corps, as follows: Longstreet's (First Corps), embracing the divisions of McLaws, Pickett, and Hood; Ewell's (Second Corps), embracing the divisions of Early, Rodes, and Johnson; and Hill's (Third Corps), embracing the divisions of Anderson, Heth, and Pender.

The last two divisions of Hill's corps were formed by adding Pettigrew's brigade, which joined the army just at that time, and J. R. Davis's brigade (formed for him by taking scattered Mississippi regiments from mixed brigades), to the six which constituted A. P. Hill's old division, and dividing the eight into two divisions of four brigades each. The army remained the same as to brigades, with the exception of the one additional under General Pettigrew. General Corse was left with his brigade of Pickett's division, and a North Carolina regiment,[1] at Hanover Junction, and took no part in the Pennsylvania campaign; his command offset the brigade brought to the army by General Pettigrew, and I therefore assume that the army return just now quoted shows General Lee's maximum strength in that campaign.

On the 20th of July, 1863, after the return of General Lee to Virginia, his army numbered forty-one thousand

[1] The Forty-fourth North Carolina, of Pettigrew's brigade.

three hundred and eighty-eight effective, *exclusive* of the cavalry corps, of which no report is made in the return of the date last mentioned; allowing seven thousand six hundred and twelve, a fair estimate for the cavalry, the effective total of the army, on the 20th of July, was forty-nine thousand. It appears, therefore, that General Lee's loss in the Pennsylvania campaign was about nineteen thousand.

Concerning the strength of the Federal army, General Meade testified as follows before the Committee on the Conduct of the War (second series, vol. i., p. 337): "Including all arms of the service, my strength was a little under one hundred thousand men—about ninety-five thousand. I think General Lee had about ninety thousand infantry, four thousand to five thousand artillery, and about ten thousand cavalry." Again he testifies: "I think the returns showed me, when I took command of the army, amounted to about one hundred and five thousand men: included in those were the eleven thousand of General French." In this latter matter the evidence is against General Meade. General Hooker, on the 27th of June, 1863, telegraphed to General Halleck, from Poolesville, "My whole force of *enlisted men* for duty will not exceed one hundred and five thousand (105,000)." This would make his total effective (officers and men) fully one hundred and twelve thousand. This dispatch [1] was received by General Halleck at 9 A. M. On reaching Sandy Hook, subsequently, on the same day, General Hooker telegraphed as follows concerning the garrison at Harper's Ferry under General French: "I find ten thousand men here in condition to take the field. Here they are of no earthly account. They cannot defend a ford of the river; and, as far as Harper's Ferry is concerned, there is nothing of it. As for the fortifications, the work of the troops, they remain when the troops are withdrawn. No enemy will ever take possession of them for them. This is my opinion. All the public property could have been secured to-night, and the troops

---

[1] "Report on the Conduct of the War," second series, vol. i., p. 291.

marched to where they could have been of some service."
This dispatch was received by General Halleck at 2.55 P. M.[1]

It is evident that the garrison at Harper's Ferry was not embraced in the returns alluded to by General Hooker, in his first dispatch. Although General Halleck refused these troops to General Hooker, they were immediately awarded to General Meade on his assuming command when General Hooker was relieved.

Without more accurate returns of the two armies at Gettysburg, we are left to form our conclusions as to their strength from the data given above. I put the Army of the Potomac at one hundred and five thousand, and the Army of Northern Virginia at sixty-two thousand of all arms—fifty thousand infantry, eight thousand cavalry, and four thousand artillery—and believe these figures very nearly correct.

In this estimate, I adopt the strength of the Federal army as given by its commander on the 27th of June, but four days before the first encounter at Gettysburg, excluding all consideration of the troops at Harper's Ferry, although General Meade, on assuming command, at once ordered General French to move to Frederick with seven thousand men, to protect his communications,[2] and thus made available a like number of men of the Army of the Potomac, who would otherwise have been detached for this service.

On the side of the Confederates, the entire cavalry corps is included. That portion which General Stuart accompanied made a complete circuit of the Federal army, and only joined General Lee on the evening of the second day; and the brigades under Generals Jones and Robertson, which had been left to guard the passes of the Blue Ridge, did not rejoin the army until the 3d of July; only the commands of Generals Imboden and Jenkins had been with the army from the time of crossing the Potomac, and they accom-

[1] "Report on the Conduct of the War," second series, vol. i., p. 292.
[2] Ibid., p. 335.

panied General Ewell. "General Stuart had several skir-
mishes during his march, and at Hanover quite a severe engagement took place with a strong force of cavalry, which
was finally compelled to withdraw from the town. The ranks
of the cavalry were much reduced by its long and arduous
march, repeated conflicts, and insufficient supplies of food
and forage." [1] I have deducted from the strength of General Lee's army, at the opening of the campaign, one month
previous to the battle, only a reasonable allowance for losses
by sickness and straggling, casualties in the encounters with
the enemy under General Milroy and in the constant skirmishing of the cavalry before and after leaving Virginia, and
the detachments left to guard our communications, to protect captured property, and to escort prisoners taken on the
Virginia side of the river.

[1] General Lee's "Report of the Pennsylvania Campaign."

CHAPTER IX.

ON the 5th of July our army left Gettysburg. Owing to the swollen condition of the Potomac, it did not recross into Virginia until the 13th of the same month; it was not, however, seriously annoyed or molested in the interval, though confidently and anxiously expecting to be attacked. In consequence of Meade's advance into Virginia east of the mountains, General Lee moved his army so as to confront him, and soon established his line of defense along the Rapidan River, where the army was allowed two months of comparative rest and quiet. In October General Lee again advanced, but no general engagement ensued. The following extracts from notes taken by me at the time will serve to illustrate the nature and extent of the movements then made :

BRISTOE STATION, *October*, 1863.

On Sunday (11th) we continued our march for Culpeper Court-House, where the enemy had been in position, with a view of reaching his flank or forcing him to retire. On arriving at a point five miles from the Court-House, we learned that Meade had taken refuge on the farther side of the Rappahannock River, and it was necessary to try another flank-movement. On Monday, therefore, we started for Warrenton by way of Warrenton Springs. On reaching the river near the latter point our progress was opposed by the enemy who held the opposite bank; but we very soon succeeded in forcing a passage at the ford. We camped near the springs that night, and passed them the next day on our way to Warrenton. On Wednesday we left Warrenton and reached this place the same day. Here Hill's advance met a corps of the enemy and at once engaged it. Our other corps came up in good time, and we should have punished the enemy severely; but matters were not properly managed and they all escaped us, and, what is worse, they got the better of us in what little fighting there was. Our people were not put into battle correctly, too few of one corps being engaged, and the other not having its line of battle in the proper direction. By unpardonable mismanagement the enemy was allowed to capture five pieces of our artillery. There was no earthly excuse for it, as all our troops were well in hand, and much stronger than the enemy.

The next morning it was discovered that the latter had retreated toward Centreville and taken refuge behind his fortifications. For the past two days we have been destroying this railroad, which is highly essential to the Federals in their "on to Richmond;" and from present indications I think that a general engagement is improbable, and that the fighting for this season is pretty much over. We have taken about fifteen hundred prisoners, forced the enemy back to Alexandria and Centreville without any general battle, and gained from him, for a time at least, a large portion of our State.

CAMP NEAR BRANDY STATION, *November* 7, 1863.

This evening the enemy advanced upon us at Kelly's Ford on the Rappahannock River, and also at Rappahannock Station; effected a crossing at the former place, rushed upon our men (two brigades) who were at the latter place defending the bridge, overwhelmed and captured most of them. Thus, in a very few words, I record the saddest chapter in the history of this army. Twelve or fifteen hundred men were captured, and also a battery of artillery of four pieces.

Reference is here made to the unfortunate affair of the *tête-de-pont* near Rappahannock bridge. At the time, great chagrin was felt at the disaster, and much discussion was had as to the responsibility therefor.

Some maintained that the place was naturally strong, and that, with the aid of the earthworks, it could be readily defended; others contended that the works were of but little protection, and the means of escape, in event of disaster, inadequate. I cannot do better, in aiding to effect a determination of these questions, than quote, from the official reports of General Lee and Major-General Early, the views they respectively entertained.

General Lee says:

To hold the line of the Rappahannock at this part of its course it was deemed advantageous to maintain our communication with the north bank, to threaten any flank-movement the enemy might make above or below, and thus compel him to divide his forces, when it was hoped that an opportunity would be presented to concentrate on one or the other part. For this purpose, a point was selected a short distance above the site of the railroad-bridge, where the hills on each side of the river afforded protection to our pontoon-bridge, and increased the means of defense. The enemy had previously constructed some small earthworks on these hills, to repel an attack from the south. That on the north side was converted into a *tête-de-pont*, and a line of rifle-trenches extended along the crest on the right and left to the river-bank. The works on the south side were remodeled, and sunken batteries for additional guns constructed on an adjacent hill to the left. Higher up on the same side and east of the railroad, near the river-bank, sunken batteries for two guns, and rifle-pits, were arranged to command the railroad embankment, under cover of which the enemy might advance. The works were slight, but were deemed adequate to accomplish the object for which they were intended. The pontoon-bridge was considered a sufficient means of communication, as, in the event of the troops north of the river being compelled to withdraw, their crossing could be covered by the artillery and infantry in the works on the south side. Four pieces of artillery were placed in the *tête-de-pont* and eight others in the works opposite.

In speaking of the assault by the enemy, he continues:

As soon, however, as it became dark enough to conceal his movements, the enemy advanced in overwhelming numbers against our rifle-trenches and succeeded in carrying them in the manner described in the reports of Generals Early and Hays. It would appear from these reports, and the short duration of the firing, that the enemy was enabled to approach very near the works before being seen. The valley in our front aided in concealing his advance from view, and a strong wind effectually prevented any movements from being heard. It was essential to the maintenance of the position, under these circumstances, that sharp-shooters should have been thrown forward to give early information of his approach, in order that he might be subjected to fire as long as possible, but it is not stated that this precaution was taken. The breaking of the enemy's first line and the surrender of part of it, as described in the reports, also contributed to divert attention from the approach of the second and third, and enabled them to press into the works. The darkness of the night, and the fear of injuring our own men who had surrendered, prevented General Early from using the artillery on the south bank. . . .

The suggestions above mentioned afford the only explanation I am able to give of this unfortunate affair, as the courage and good conduct of the troops engaged have been too often tried to admit of any question.

The loss of this position made it necessary to abandon the design of attacking the force that had crossed at Kelly's Ford, and the army was withdrawn to the only tenable line between Culpeper Court-House and the Rappahannock, where it remained during the succeeding day. The position not being regarded as favorable, it returned the night following to the south side of the Rapidan.

General Early, whose division alternated with that under

General Johnson in furnishing a garrison for the works, and whose troops were on duty the day in question, says:

The works on the north side of the river were, in my judgment, very inadequate and not judiciously laid out or constructed. . . . There was no ditch on the outside of the work. . . . I had myself pointed out some of the defects of the works to the engineers having charge of them, and I had urged the necessity of having another bridge farther up the stream. The fact is, in my opinion, the position was susceptible of being made very strong, but, in order to enable a small force to hold it against a large attacking force, the works ought to have been entirely inclosed, and with a deep ditch on the outside, so that an attacking column could have had its progress checked. But the works were so constructed as to afford no obstacle in themselves to an attacking enemy, and only furnished a temporary protection to our troops. . . . In a short time some firing of musketry at and in front of the rifle-trenches was observed from the flashes of the guns, it being impossible to hear the report by reason of the wind, though the distance was but short. After this firing had continued for some minutes it slackened somewhat, and, not hearing from it, we were of opinion that it was from and at the enemy's skirmishers.

The works were quickly overrun, and, as before stated, the greater part of two brigades was captured, as also the four pieces of artillery in the *tête-de-pont*. After this the pontoon-bridge was burned.

CAMP NEAR BRANDY STATION, *November* 7, 1863.

We are all packed up and will move to-night. We are now in the line of outposts, and this is not exactly the place for the commanding general. No sleep to-night, and to-morrow an active, stirring Sunday. How singular it is that most of our battles and movements occur on that day, when, of all others, we should most enjoy quiet and be most reminded of peace !

I think that General Meade means to fight, and General Lee will accommodate him, but on ground of his own choosing.

The movements here alluded to only resulted in both armies being reëstablished in their old lines along the Rapidan River, without an engagement.

CAMP NEAR ORANGE, *November* 26, 1863.

We are just on the eve of another move. This morning and afternoon all the indications favor the supposition that the enemy is moving down the river, and we have been busy preparing for a counter-move in the same direction. Matters seem to be drifting toward our old and renowned battle-fields, Chancellorsville and Fredericksburg. The enemy occupies the line of the Rapidan on the north side, we on the south side. He will in all probability move to Germania Ford, near the confluence of the Rappahannock and the Rapidan, where he will cross. Then, as we will be advancing in that direction, there will be a clash somewhere between that point and Fredericksburg. We have all our arrangements made to move before dawn in the morning.

CAMP NEAR ORANGE, *December*, 1863.

By the dawn of day on the 27th of last month, we were many miles from Orange on our way to meet Meade's army, which had crossed to the south side of the Rapidan. It was intensely cold. We left camp at 3 A. M.—as usual, the general was ahead of every one else—and we arrived at Verdiersville without any army whatever, the troops not having progressed that far. During the morning the army caught up with us, and we proceeded to advance toward Fredericksburg. In the afternoon we first met the enemy; on the right there was a little skirmishing; on the left, Johnson's division engaged and severely chastised a corps of the enemy; at the same time our cavalry, under General Rosser, attacked and destroyed a large ordnance-train in the enemy's rear. With the exception of one other cavalry affair, no more fighting of any consequence occurred. On Saturday we selected our position on the line of Mine Run, and proceeded to fortify it. In an incredibly short time (for our men work now like beavers) we were strongly intrenched, and ready and anxious for an attack. The general gave his attention to the whole line—directing important changes here and

there; endeavoring to impress the officers with the importance
of success in the impending engagement; and presenting a fine
example of untiring energy and zeal. He was busy the whole
time.

On Sunday, as we were riding down the lines, attended by
General Hill with his staff and others, we came upon a collec-
tion of men engaged in divine worship. We had been riding at
a pretty fair gait, but the general at once halted, and listened
to the singing of the men. He heard the entire hymn, and as
the benediction was pronounced, reverently raised his hat from
his head, received the blessing, and then continued his ride
along the fortifications. It was a striking scene, and one well
calculated to impress solemnly all who witnessed it. The para-
pet was crowded with men; here and there at proper intervals
waved the battle-flags; and from many dozen embrasures
frowned the now silent artillery. This all looked exceedingly
warlike, and it was a cheering thing to see that, while ready for
action, our men did not forget that, to secure victory, divine
help should be implored.

On Monday we confidently looked for an attack. It passed
without one. The enemy was in our immediate front, and he,
too, had intrenched. This looked rather queer, to see two large
armies face to face, each busily constructing works for defense.

Tuesday came and went without an attack. General Lee
had now become impatient, and, seeing how reluctant the enemy
was to bring on an engagement, he determined to relieve him of
further embarrassment by becoming the aggressor, and forcing
him into a fight. Consequently, during the night two fine
divisions were relieved from the trenches and concentrated on
our right, ready to be thrown on the enemy's left flank; other
necessary arrangements for a grand battle were completed
before morning.

Information received during the night indicated some activity
in the enemy's lines, and at dawn of day it was found that he
had fled, and was fast making his way back toward the river.
Pursuit was immediately ordered and made; but General Meade
had too much the advance of us, and reached the north side of
the Rapidan before we could overtake him. Both armies then

retired to their original positions. Undoubtedly we were most benefited by the movement. We captured about seven hundred prisoners, four hundred mules and horses, and destroyed or secured one hundred and twenty or one hundred and thirty wagons; the enemy's loss in killed and wounded will reach perhaps one thousand. So, all things considered, we may be said to have canceled Bristoe Station. It was an almost bloodless victory; for we enjoy all the moral effects of a victory, without its usual and distressing losses. General Meade expected either to take us unawares, turn our flank, and force us from behind the fortifications on the Rapidan, or else he concluded that, as soon as he crossed, General Lee would retreat to Hanover Junction; but our general is not so easily frightened into a retreat, and can very readily change his front.

Both armies remained in a state of comparative inaction during the months of January and February, 1864, until the 28th day of the latter month, when a powerful cavalry expedition, embracing three columns, under Kilpatrick, Dahlgren, and Custer, started from the Federal lines with the avowed purpose of capturing and sacking the city of Richmond. At this time General Lee was at Richmond. The indications of the advance of Custer's column on our left, received at army headquarters on the evening of the 28th, were confirmed on the 29th, when the whole movement was fully developed. The route of this column was to have been *via* Charlottesville, at which point there was no Confederate force, and the country intervening was filled with our artillery and wagon camps. Upon the receipt of the first intelligence of this movement on the evening of the 28th, all the trains moving in the direction of the threatened route were diverted. On the 29th a force of infantry was dispatched by rail to Charlottesville; but the advance of the enemy operating on this flank was effectually checked before reaching that place by our horse-artillery and dismounted cavalry.

The column which moved upon our right, under Kilpatrick, was more successful. The entire Confederate cavalry picket stationed at Eley's Ford was captured; and this column of the enemy reached the Central Railroad before any intelligence was received of its advance. After cutting the road, it proceeded toward Richmond. General Lee returned to the army on the last train, which passed up but a few hours before the enemy reached the road, and thus barely escaped capture. The fate of this column, and especially of that portion of it commanded by Colonel Dahlgren, is well known. The results were most disastrous to the Federals, including the death of that officer, and the capture of his orders, exposing the damaging fact of the intention of the enemy to pillage and burn the city and kill the most prominent Confederate officials.

Early in April General Lee was directed to inquire of General Meade, by flag of truce, if he or his Government sanctioned what Colonel Dahlgren had proposed and ordered in his address to his troops. On the 18th of April a reply to this communication was received, to the effect that neither General Meade, General Kilpatrick, nor the authorities at Washington, ordered or approved the burning of Richmond, the killing of Mr. Davis and his cabinet, or anything else not rendered necessary by military causes or not legitimate in civilized warfare. General Kilpatrick stated that the photographic copy of the " address" which had been received through General Lee was a fac-simile of an address which Colonel Dahlgren had submitted to him for his approval, and which he had approved in red ink, *except* that it lacked that approval and contained the objectionable exhortations or orders, which were not in that submitted to him. The disclaimer of General Meade was most candid and emphatic.

Information was received, about the latter part of April, of the advance of the Ninth (Federal) Corps from the neighborhood of Annapolis to reënforce General Grant, who had now assumed command of the Army of the Potomac.

CHAPTER X.

General Grant in Command of the Federal Army of the Potomac.—His Advance.
—From the Wilderness to Petersburg.—Strength of the Two Armies.

By reference to the official returns of the Army of Northern Virginia,[1] I find that on the 20th of April, 1864, the Second Corps reported seventeen thousand and seventy-nine and the Third Corps twenty-two thousand one hundred and ninety-nine present for duty; there were also two unattached commands—viz., the Maryland line and the Provost Guard, numbering together eleven hundred and twenty-five effective. Two divisions of the First Corps had but recently arrived from Tennessee, and were not embraced in this return. I am without certain information as to their strength at that time. When the First Corps was detached for service in Tennessee, the effective strength of its *three* divisions was fourteen thousand six hundred and sixty-eight (*see* return of August 31, 1863). After the hard service in the West, I am sure that the two divisions under Generals Field and Kershaw, when they rejoined the army, could not have exceeded ten thousand effective. With this liberal estimate, it appears that General Lee's total infantry force was fifty thousand four hundred and three; to which if we add the cavalry corps, eight thousand seven hundred and twenty-seven, and the artillery corps, four thousand eight hundred and fifty-four, as given in the same return, we have a total present for duty, of all arms, of sixty-three thousand nine hundred and

[1] Now on file in the Archive-Office, War Department, Washington, D. C.

eighty-four—in round numbers say sixty-four thousand men —under General Lee, at the opening of the campaign of 1864.

The official return of the Army of the Potomac of the 1st of May, 1864, shows present for duty one hundred and twenty thousand three hundred and eighty men of all arms; to which if we add the Ninth Corps, not embraced in this return, but which joined General Grant before he commenced active operations, and which numbered, according to official returns, twenty thousand seven hundred and eighty, we have a total of one hundred and forty-one thousand one hundred and sixty men of all arms under General Grant at the opening of the campaign.[1]

I have given the relative strength of the two armies at the outset of this campaign, in order that the reader, in following the course of events, may have a proper appreciation of the difficulties which beset General Lee in the task of thwarting the designs of so formidable an adversary, and realize the extent to which his brilliant genius made amends for paucity of numbers, and proved more than a match for brute force, as illustrated in the hammering policy of General Grant.

If one hundred and forty thousand men are made to grapple in a death-struggle with sixty thousand men, of the former twenty thousand should survive the total annihilation of the latter, even though the price exacted for such destruction be in the ratio of two for one. Behold the theory of the Federal commander and an epitome of his conception of *strategy*, as exemplified on the sanguinary field extending from the Wilderness to James River!

On the 4th day of May General Grant opened the campaign by crossing to the south side of the Rapidan River, with the intention of placing his army between that of General Lee and Richmond, his objective point.

---

[1] These figures are taken from the " Report of the Secretary of War to the First Session of the Thirty-ninth Congress," vol. i., 1865–'66, pp. 3–5, 55.

General Lee was fully aware of the great disparity in the strength of the two armies, and of the efforts that had been made, under General Grant's direction, to increase the efficiency of the Army of the Potomac by every possible means, and it was doubtless expected that he would hesitate to give battle against such fearful odds, and proceed to manœuvre to avoid a general engagement, and, by " masterly retreat," retard the progress of his adversary.

The Federal commanders should by this time have learned to expect, with moral certainty, that, just as soon as they emerged from their own lines, there was an arm uplifted that would inevitably fall upon them with the speed of lightning and with tremendous power.

So soon as the real design of General Grant was disclosed, General Lee advanced to attack him. It was, indeed, a bold movement; but, strange to relate, it appears not to have been expected by the enemy. Moving down on the south side of the Rapidan, the Army of Northern Virginia soon encountered its old adversary, under its new commander, in the Wilderness, and, without parley or delay, grappled it, and took the initiative in what was destined to be a prolonged and bitter struggle.

General Grant, who had started for a march, found it necessary to concentrate for battle. Much hard fighting ensued: for two days there was a murderous wrestle; severe and rapid blows were given and received in turn, until sheer exhaustion called a truce, with the advantage on the Confederate side. Notably was this the case in a brilliant assault made by General Longstreet on the Federal left on the 6th of May; and in a turning movement on their right on the same day, executed by a portion of General Ewell's (Second) corps—the brigades of Gordon, Johnston, and Pegram—doubling up that flank and forcing it back a considerable distance.

Mention should also be made of the stubborn and heroic resistance, on the 5th of May, by the divisions of Heth and

Wilcox of Hill's (Third) corps—fifteen thousand strong[1]— against the repeated and desperate assaults of five divisions of the enemy—the four divisions of Hancock's corps and one of Sedgwick's—numbering about forty-five thousand men, in which the Confederates completely foiled their adversaries, and inflicted upon them most serious loss.[2]

The Third Division of Hill's (Third) corps, under General Anderson, and the two divisions of Longstreet's (First) corps, did not reach the scene of conflict until dawn of day on the morning of the 6th. Simultaneously the attack on Hill was renewed with great vigor. In addition to the force which he had so successfully resisted the previous day, a fresh division of the Fifth Corps, under General Wadsworth, had secured position on his flank, and coöperated with the column assaulting in front. After a short contest, the divisions of Heth and Wilcox, who had expected to be relieved, and were not prepared for the enemy's assault, were overpowered and compelled to retire, just as the advance of Longstreet's column reached the ground. The defeated divisions were in considerable disorder, and the condition of affairs was exceedingly critical. General Lee fully appreciated the impending crisis, and, dashing amid the fugitives, personally called upon the men to rally. General Longstreet, taking in the situation at a glance, was prompt to act—immediately caused his divisions to be deployed in line of battle, and gallantly advanced to recover the lost ground.

The soldiers, seeing General Lee's manifest purpose to advance with them, and realizing the great danger in which he then was, called upon him in a beseeching manner to "go

---

[1] " Return of the Army of Northern Virginia," April 20, 1864, chap. xiv.

[2] The troops engaged in this assault were, Getty's division (four brigades) of the Sixth Corps ; Hancock's corps—viz., Birney's division (two brigades), Mott's division (two brigades), Gibbon's division (three brigades), and Barlow's division (four brigades) : in all, fifteen brigades. The Army of the Potomac embraced but thirty-two brigades, and numbered near one hundred thousand infantry. I therefore estimate that the fifteen brigades here engaged numbered forty-five thousand men.—(*See* Swinton's " Army of the Potomac," pp. 425, 426.)

to the rear," promising that they would soon have matters rectified, and begging him to retire from a position in which his life was so exposed. The general was evidently touched and gratified at this manifestation of interest and anxiety on the part of his brave men, and waved them on, with some words of cheer. Their advance under such circumstances was simply irresistible; every man felt that the eye of the commanding general was upon him, and was proud of the opportunity of showing him that his trust in his men was not misplaced. The Federal advance was checked, and the Confederate lines reëstablished.

Not content with this, as soon as the proper dispositions could be made, General Longstreet, as before mentioned, took the offensive, and assailed, with great impetuosity, the force which had overwhelmed Hill's divisions. The Federals were in turn soon compelled to yield all the ground heretofore gained, and, upon being further pressed, to fall back for shelter to a line of works some distance in rear of the line, held by them the day previous, and which had been constructed for the protection of the Brock Road, along which one of their columns advanced on the 4th of May.

So far, complete success had crowned General Longstreet's movement. The necessary orders were given by him to follow up the advantage gained, and dispositions were made to press the dismayed and fleeing enemy. Surely a decisive victory was now to be vouchsafed the Confederate arms, when, lo! by an accident truly calamitous in its results, the Confederates were deprived of their leader. General Longstreet, with his staff, was advancing along the road at the head of Jenkins's brigade, when the latter—mistaken for a body of the enemy by a portion of the flanking column, which continued its advance through the woods—was fired into. General Longstreet was seriously wounded, and General Jenkins fell dead. The forward movement was checked, and thus was time afforded the Federals in which to rally, reënforce, and reform, behind their intrenchments. Thus, by a strange fatality, a second time was Lee's lieutenant stricken down in the tangled mazes of the Wilderness, when in the full tide of victory, and that not by hostile hand!

In these encounters in the Wilderness the Confederates inflicted severe losses upon the enemy, and, besides gaining ground, captured prisoners, artillery, and other trophies. As can be well understood, these results were attained, however, at serious cost to General Lee, who, constrained to spare his men as much as possible, hesitated to assail the enemy in his intrenched position, and hopefully awaited attack. General Grant did not again assume the aggressive, and so the 7th passed in comparative quiet.

General Grant, in pursuance of his original design, then attempted, by a rapid flank movement, to secure possession of Spottsylvania Court-House; but General Lee, on the night of the 7th, anticipated his purpose, and detached a portion of Longstreet's corps, under command of General R. H. Anderson, to move at once to that point. The van of the opposing forces, each making for the same goal, arrived almost simultaneously on the morning of the 8th at the Court-House. The Federals, a little in advance, drove back the Confederate cavalry, but were in turn quickly dispossessed of the strategic point by the opportune arrival of Anderson's infantry. The two armies then swung round, each forming on its advanced guard as a nucleus, and on the 9th confronted each other in line of battle.

General Lee was still between his adversary and Richmond. These movements were necessarily made with great rapidity, and the several commands, as they moved into line, proceeded at once to fortify in the positions in which they found themselves, without due regard to a perfect alignment, and ignoring to a certain extent natural advantages and disadvantages. The line of defense, as thus originally constructed, was consequently imperfect, and at some points quite vulnerable.

On the 10th of May, by a spirited dash, the enemy made

a lodgment on the left of General Ewell, obtaining temporary possession of a portion of the lines and a battery of
artillery. It was there again that General Lee started for the
breach, with the purpose of leading the troops in the effort
to regain the lost ground, when his staff and other officers
surrounded him and urged him to desist, imploring him not
thus to expose himself to an almost certain death. To their
expostulations he replied that he would relinquish his purpose if they would see to it that the lines were reëstablished
—that that "must be done." And it was done! The
enemy was quickly made to relinquish his temporary advantage, and both guns and ground were recovered.

Upon an examination of the lines, General Lee had de-
tected the weakness of that portion known as "the salient,"
to the right of the point assailed on the 10th, to which I have
just alluded, and occupied by the division of General Edward
Johnson (Ewell's corps), and had directed a second line to be
constructed across its base, to which he proposed to move
back the troops occupying the angle. These arrangements
were not quite completed, when he thought he saw cause to
suspect another flank-movement by General Grant, and, on
the night of the 11th, ordered most of the artillery at this
portion of the lines to be withdrawn, so as to be available to
take part in a counter-movement. Toward the dawn of day,
on the 12th, General Johnson discovered indications of an
impending assault upon his front. He sent immediate orders
for the return of his artillery, and caused other preparations
for defense to be made; but the enemy, who could advance
without discovery to within a short distance of the works
under cover of a body of woods, had massed there a large
force, and, with the advent of the first rays of morning light,
by a spirited assault, quickly overran that portion of the lines
before the artillery could be put in position, and captured
most of the division, including its brave commander. The
army was thus cut in twain, and the situation was one well
calculated to test the skill of its commander and the nerve

and courage of the men. Dispositions were immediately made to repair the breach, and troops were moved up from the right and left to dispute the further progress of the assaulting column. Then occurred the most remarkable musketry-fire of the war: from the sides of the salient, in the possession of the Federals, and the new line, forming the base of the triangle, occupied by the Confederates, poured forth, from continuous lines of hissing fire, an incessant, terrific hail of deadly missiles. No living man nor thing could stand in the doomed space embraced within those angry lines; even large trees were felled—their trunks cut in twain by the bullets of small-arms. Never did the troops on either side display greater valor and determination. Intense and bitter was the struggle. The Confederates, moving up to fill the gap, fell with tremendous power upon the Federal mass, caused it to recoil somewhat, closed with it in a hand-to-hand conflict, but failed to dislodge it; while the Federal assault, which threatened such serious consequences, was effectually checked, and the advantage to the enemy resulting therefrom was limited to the possession of the narrow space of the salient and the capture of the force which had occupied it. The loss of this fine body of troops was seriously felt by General Lee; but sadly reduced though his army was, by this and a week's incessant fighting, such was the metal of what remained that his lines, thus forcibly rectified, proved thereafter impregnable.

Several days of comparative quiet ensued. The army under General Grant was at this time heavily reënforced from Washington. In his official report of this campaign he says, " The 13th, 14th, 15th, 16th, 17th, and 18th (of May), were consumed in manœuvring and awaiting the arrival of reënforcements from Washington." [1] In numerical strength his army so much exceeded that under General Lee that, after covering the entire Confederate front with double lines

[1] General Grant's " Report," " Report of the Secretary of War to the Thirty-ninth Congress," vol. ii., p. 1106.

of battle, he had in reserve a large force with which to extend his flank, and compel a corresponding movement on the part of his adversary, in order to keep between him and his coveted prize—the capital of the Confederacy.

On the 18th another assault was directed against the Confederate lines, but it produced no impression. No effort was made after this—the task was a hopeless one, and was reluctantly relinquished.

On the night of the 20th, General Grant started on another flank-movement in the direction of Bowling Green. General Lee in order to intercept him moved to Hanover Junction.

I again make one or two extracts from notes taken at the time, as illustrating the spirit of the army and the character of the work it was called on to perform:

CAMP AT HANOVER JUNCTION, *May* 23, 1864.

. . . . For the first time since the 4th of the month we were on yesterday spared the sight of the enemy. On the day before it was discovered that he was leaving our front and moving toward Bowling Green. He dared not, as we prayed he would, attack us again at Spottsylvania. With several rivers between his army and ours, he could move to Bowling Green and below without any danger of our intercepting him. He would thus get some miles nearer Richmond, in a geographical sense, but in reality be as far from that city as ever, because this army will still confront him, let him change his base as often as he pleases. To counteract his new design, our army was put in motion for this place. The enemy had the start of us, but by excellent marching we have again placed him in our front. It is probable that he will make still another move to our right, and land somewhere near West Point.

This would of course necessitate our moving between that point and Richmond. Why General Grant did not carry his army to his new base without incurring the heavy losses he has sustained in battle, I cannot say. If Fredericksburg was his destination, he could have attained possession of it without the loss of a hundred men. The same can be said of West Point. After his discomfiture in the Wilderness, he started for Spottsylvania Court-House, hoping to reach there before General Lee. There were but few indications of his intended departure from our front at that time to most of us, but General Lee seemed to divine his intention, and sent a corps to Spottsylvania just in time to meet the enemy at that place. We engaged them and beat them back, thereby securing the Court-House. In commenting upon this, the Northern papers say that we retreated and that Grant pursued us ; while the truth is, General Grant was completely outgeneraled. No doubt the entire North is this day rejoicing over our retreat to this point; yet the battle-field was left in our possession, and we marched here without any molestation whatever. This does not look like a retreat. Our army is in excellent condition ; its *morale* as good as when we met Grant—two weeks since—for the first time. He will feel us again before he reaches his prize. His losses have been already fearfully large. Our list of casualties is a sad one to contemplate, but does not compare with his terrible record of killed and wounded : he does not pretend to bury his dead, leaves his wounded without proper attendance, and seems entirely reckless as regards the lives of his men. This, and his remarkable pertinacity, constitute his sole claim to superiority over his predecessors. He certainly holds on longer than any of them. He alone, of all, would have remained this side of the Rapidan after the battles of the Wilderness.

The gage of battle proffered by General Lee at Hanover Junction was declined by General Grant, who, in order to extricate his army from a position of some embarrassment, about the 26th of May, recrossed to the north side of the North Anna River, and made another *détour* to the east. General Lee moved upon a parallel line. If his army had been of even reasonable proportions in comparison with that of his adversary, his movement would have been of another character, and one of the two wings of the Federal army would have been assailed while on the south side of the river.

On the 30th of May General Lee was in line of battle, with his left at Atlee's Station.

CAMP AT ATLEE'S STATION, *early Morning*, *May* 30, 1864.

. . . . We are confronting General Grant, and only waiting to have him located—to have his position well developed—before this army is let loose at its old opponent. On yesterday afternoon the enemy appeared to be advancing toward us, and this morning I confidently expected to hear the firing of small-arms before this hour. . . . We have now had three weeks of constant fighting, marching, and watching. . . .

The general has been somewhat indisposed, and could attend to nothing except what was absolutely necessary for him to know and act upon. . . . He is now improving.

The indisposition of General Lee here alluded to was more serious than was generally supposed. Those near him were very apprehensive lest he should be compelled to give up. To quote the words of one of his greatest admirers and most trusted friends, Lieutenant-General Early :

One of his three corps commanders had been disabled by wounds at the Wilderness, and another was too sick to command his corps, while he himself was suffering from a most annoying and weakening disease. In fact, nothing but his own determined will enabled him to keep the field at all ; and it was there rendered more manifest than ever that he was the head and front, the very life and soul of his army.

After feeling the Confederate position, attack was declined by the enemy. By another gyratory movement of the kind so persistently pursued by General Grant in this campaign, the two armies again gravitated east, and were soon (June 3d) face to face on the historic field of Cold Harbor. Here, gallant but fruitless efforts were made by General Grant to pierce or drive back the army under General Lee. The Confederates were protected by temporary earthworks, and while under cover of these were gallantly assailed by the Federals. But in vain : the assault was repulsed along the whole line, and the carnage on the Federal side was frightful. I well recall having received a report after the assault from General Hoke—whose division reached the army just previous to this battle—to the effect that the ground in his entire front, over which the enemy had charged, was literally covered with their dead and wounded ; and that up to that time he had not had a single man killed. No wonder that, when the command was given to renew the assault, the Federal soldiers sullenly and silently declined to advance.[1] After some disingenuous proposals, General Grant finally asked a truce to enable him to bury his dead. Soon after this he abandoned his chosen line of operations, and moved his army to the south side of James River. The struggle from the Wilderness to this point covered a period of over one month ; during which time there had been an almost daily encounter of hostile arms, and the Army of Northern Virginia had placed *hors de combat* of the army under General Grant a number equal to its entire numerical strength at the commencement of the campaign, and, notwithstanding its own heavy losses and the reënforcements received by the enemy, still presented an impregnable front to its opponent, and constituted an insuperable barrier to General Grant's " On to Richmond ! "

After an unsuccessful effort to surprise and capture Petersburg—which was prevented by the skill of Generals Beauregard and Wise, and the bravery of the troops, consisting in part of militia and home-guards—and a futile endeavor to seize the Richmond & Petersburg Railroad, General Grant concentrated his army south of the Appomattox River. General Lee, whom he had not been able to defeat in the

[1] " The order was issued through these officers to their subordinate commanders, and from them descended through the wonted channels ; but no man stirred, and the immobile lines pronounced a verdict, silent, yet emphatic, against further slaughter. The loss on the Union side in this sanguinary action was over thirteen thousand, while on the part of the Confederates it is doubtful whether it reached that many hundreds."—(Swinton, " Army of the Potomac," p. 487.)

open field, was still in his way, and the siege of Petersburg was begun.

General Lee was compelled about this time to detach General Early, with the Second Corps, to check the advance of the Federal force under General Hunter that was moving up the Valley, laying waste as it advanced and threatening our communications with the interior *via* Lynchburg. It will be well understood that he could not spare any portion of his army, already greatly inferior in numerical strength to its opponent, but no other troops were available.

It has been seen that, at the commencement of this extraordinary campaign, the effective strength of the army under General Lee was sixty-four thousand men, and that under General Grant one hundred and forty-one thousand one hundred and sixty men. The only reënforcements received by General Lee were as follows: Near Hanover Junction he was joined by a small force under General Breckinridge, from Southwestern Virginia, twenty-two hundred strong, and Pickett's division of Longstreet's (First) corps, which had been on detached service in North Carolina; Hoke's brigade of Early's division, twelve hundred strong, which had been on detached duty at the Junction, here also rejoined its division; and at Cold Harbor General Lee received the division of General Hoke, also just from North Carolina—the two divisions (Pickett's and Hoke's) numbering eleven thousand men.[1] The aggregate of these reënforcements (fourteen thousand four hundred men) added to General Lee's original strength would give seventy-eight thou-

[1] The " Monthly Return of General Lee's Army," of the 30th of June, 1864, shows that at that date Pickett's division numbered four thousand eight hundred and eighty-four, and Hoke's division five thousand two hundred and eighty-six, making together ten thousand one hundred and seventy effective. Hoke was engaged at Cold Harbor, but suffered little loss ; Pickett lost a few hundred men in his assault on the enemy's lines between the James and Appomattox Rivers on the 16th of June. The joint loss of the two divisions did not exceed eight hundred men between the time they joined General Lee and the date of the return quoted.

sand four hundred as the aggregate of all troops engaged under him from the Wilderness to Cold Harbor.

When at Spottsylvania Court-House General Grant was reënforced from Washington, but I can only conjecture to what extent. The Secretary of War states that "the chief part of the force designed to guard the Middle Department and the Department of Washington was called forward to the front"[1] at this time. The same authority puts the effective strength of these two departments on the 1st of May at forty-seven thousand seven hundred and fifty-one men,[2] of which the chief part—let us say, thirty-five thousand—was sent to the aid of General Grant. At Cold Harbor he was joined by General W. F. Smith with four divisions, taken from the Tenth and Eighteenth Corps, numbering sixteen thousand men.[3] Adding these reënforcements to General Grant's original strength, we have one hundred and ninety-two thousand one hundred and sixty men as the aggregate of the troops employed by him in his operations from the Rapidan to the James.

The Federal loss in the battles of the Wilderness, Spottsylvania, North Anna, and Cold Harbor, is put at "above sixty thousand men" by Mr. Swinton in his history of the "Army of the Potomac."

[1] "Report of the Secretary of War, First Session, Thirty-ninth Congress," vol. i., 1865–'66, p. 7.
[2] Ibid., pp. 5, 6.
[3] Swinton, "Army of the Potomac," p. 482.

CHAPTER XI.

HAVING failed to obtain possession of Petersburg by surprise, and General Lee being now well established in his line
of defense, General Grant determined upon the method of
slow approaches, and proceeded to invest the city and its
brave defenders by a line of earthworks and mines. While
with his constantly-increasing numbers General Grant undertook to tighten the ligature thus applied to the carotid artery
of the Confederacy, General Sherman was sent upon his des-
olating expedition through the States of Georgia and South
Carolina to add the policy of *starvation* to that of *attrition*
inaugurated a few months previous. After this manner it
was proposed to exhaust and wear out the people who could
not be beaten in a trial of arms. It is beyond the scope of
my undertaking to record, in detail, the events and incidents
of that ten months' siege. Reduced in numbers as was the
Army of Northern Virginia, and limited as it was in supplies of all kinds, it nevertheless dealt many vigorous and
destructive blows to its adversary, and contributed much to
its already imperishable renown. I note as especially worthy of mention the recapture of our lines, after the explosion of the Federal mine at the "Crater," by the troops under General Mahone, and the many brilliant sorties made
under the direction of that gallant soldier upon the Federal

left near the Weldon road; the very successful attack on Hancock, at Reams's Station, by Heth's division and a portion of Wilcox's, on the 25th of August, under the direction of General A. P. Hill; as also the bold and successful exploits of our cavalry under General Hampton; the final charge made upon the Federal lines by General Gordon's troops, on the 25th of March; and, last but not least, the heroic defense of Fort Gregg, on the 2d of April, by a mixed command of infantry and dismounted artillery—drivers armed with muskets.

In chronological order it is well here to mention a matter about which there has been some misapprehension in the public mind. Reference is made to the part taken by General Lee in the removal of General Johnston from the command of the Army of Tennessee. In the early part of July a telegram was received by General Lee from the President, stating that a heavy pressure was being brought to bear upon him for the removal of General Johnston, asking his views in regard to it, and what he thought of the appointment of General Hood to the command of that army. The reply of General Lee was, in substance, that, while he regarded General Hood as a most capable and deserving officer, he could not recommend the change proposed; and that, in his judgment, it would be unwise, under the circumstances then existing, to make any change in commanders. The telegraphic communication between the President and General Lee was conducted in *cipher* in all matters of importance. The duty of interpreting these dispatches and putting them into *cipher* devolved upon me, and their contents were more positively and permanently impressed upon my memory than would have been the case in the mere reading or copying of an ordinary message.

Conscious that it would be unbecoming on my part to express any opinion concerning the order of the President directing the change alluded to, I touch upon this delicate matter only as it concerns General Lee, and not with the de-

sire of adding a feather's weight to the arguments for or
against the wisdom or propriety of the order relieving General Johnston of command, save that which my former comrades in arms will attach to the opinion of General Lee.

Reverting to the notes from which I have previously
quoted, I append additional extracts, whose only value, if
any they have, is derived from the fact that they were written by one who was brought into daily and intimate relations
with General Lee, and whose position made him thoroughly
informed as to all matters of routine in the Army of Northern Virginia ; and, therefore, their tone may be regarded as
in some measure indicative of the spirit and temper of that
army ; and the intimations of contemplated changes or probable movements therein made, as the reflex of the views and
opinions of General Lee as to what was regarded as expedient or probable :

NEAR PETERSBURG, VA., *August* 28, 1864.

We have had some irregular but quite severe fighting during the past two weeks, and in summing up the result there is
a decided balance in our favor.   Still, the enemy retains possession of the Weldon Railroad.   To do this, however, has cost
General Grant about twelve thousand men.

NORTH SIDE JAMES RIVER, *October* 27, 1864.

There are indications of a general movement.   The enemy
is in motion at all points.   We may have to move any moment.
General Hill, at Petersburg, reports the enemy making a general
advance on his right.   General Longstreet here reports a dem-
onstration along his entire line, and there is some activity on
the river and between the James and Appomattox.   The general has gone to the lines alone.

NORTH SIDE, *November* 1, 1864.

The general informed me last night that he wished to go to
Petersburg, and, as he would probably remain a week or more,
it would be necessary to take everything along with us.   He
has gone ahead, and will take a ride by Pickett's line.

On leaving the north side the general left it to me to select an abiding-place for our party here. I, of course, selected a place where I thought he would be comfortable, although I firmly believe he concluded that I was thinking more of myself than of him. I took possession of a vacant house and had his room prepared, with a cheerful fire, and everything made as cozy as possible. It was entirely too pleasant for him, for he is never so uncomfortable as when comfortable. A day or two after our arrival he informed me that he desired to visit the cavalry-lines, and thought it best to move our camp down. So we packed up bag and baggage—books and records—and moved to a point about eight miles distant, pitched our tents, and concluded that we were fixed for some days at least. The next morning, however, the general concluded that we had better return. So back I came to Petersburg, and as I could find no better place—nor a *worse* one that was suitable—I returned to the house we had vacated, where we are now comfortably established. This is the first time we have been quartered in a house.

While General Lee was in Richmond, I concluded to move headquarters, as a party that proposed to occupy the house as soon as we should vacate had given a gentle hint by sending to inquire " when General Lee would leave the house." The only other house available was one two miles from the city, kindly offered by the owner, Mr. Turnbull. So here we are at " Edge Hill." I am finely fixed in the parlor with piano, sofas, rocking-chairs, and pictures; capital surroundings for a winter campaign. After locating the general and my associates of the staff, I concluded that I would have to occupy one of the miserable little back-rooms, but the gentleman of the house suggested that I should take the parlor. I think that the general was pleased with his room, and on entering mine he remarked: " Ah! you are finely fixed. Couldn't you find any other room?" " No," I replied, " but *this will do*. I can make myself tolerably comfortable here." He was struck dumb with amazement at my impudence, and soon vanished.

EDGE HILL, *December* 4, 1864.

Since the affair at Stony Creek we have had perfect quiet on
our lines. The Sixth Corps, which has been with Sheridan in
General Early's front, has started for City Point—so we are informed by telegraph. General Gracie, who showed such tact in
getting General Lee to descend from a dangerous position, was
killed near the lines a day or so ago. He was an excellent
officer, had passed through many hard-fought battles, escaped
numberless dangers, and was finally killed while quietly viewing
the enemy from a point where no one dreamed of danger. I
have just received a telegram from General Ewell reporting
great commotion on the part of the enemy in his front this
evening. Movements tend to Fort Harrison.

EDGE HILL, *December* 12, 1864.

We have had much excitement during the past week; nor
has the end yet come. Couriers were arriving during the whole
of last night—and what a bitter cold night it was! So far the
enemy have accomplished but little. The whole movement
seems to have been a grand raid on the Weldon Railroad, and,
although the bridge was saved by the valor of our troops, the
enemy succeeded in destroying about ten miles of the road.
There were other movements along the lines, but in results they
were trifling. Last night another advance was reported, but it
was probably only reënforcements going to the rescue of the
first column.

EDGE HILL, *December* 18, 1864.

We have had comparative quiet since the recent affair on
the Weldon road. It is difficult to anticipate events now, but
it appears more probable that the vicinity of *Wilmington,
North Carolina, will be the scene of the next engagement* than
either Petersburg or Richmond.

EDGE HILL, *February* 5, 1865.

Instead of a quiet Sunday, we have had one of considerable
excitement: the indications are that General Grant is once more
moving on us. It is not positively known whether or not he
has been reënforced by General Thomas, but, all things consid-

ered, it is better that we should fight *now than later*. The present movement is probably a raid upon our railroads—the South Side and the Richmond & Danville. We are sanguine, and never expect anything but success; but the approaching spring campaign will be a trying one. Sherman may occasion us a great deal of trouble, and it may be necessary *to make very important changes in the campaign, and for this army to change its position.*

EDGE HILL, *February* 6, 1865.

After all, yesterday's excitement resulted in but little. The enemy have not gone after our railroads, having been checked at Dinwiddie Court-House. They have extended their lines somewhat, but as yet show no disposition to attack in force. Richmond is doubtless much excited over the return of the Peace Commission and the result of its mission. Our people now know what they have to expect.

EDGE HILL, *February* 20, 1865.

Truly matters are becoming serious and exciting. If somebody doesn't arrest Sherman's march, where will he stop? They are trying to corner this old army, but like a brave lion brought to bay at last it is determined to resist to the death, and if die it must to die game. We are to have some hard knocks, we are to experience much that is dispiriting, but if our men are true (and I really believe that most of them are) we will make our way successfully through the dark clouds that now surround us. *Our people must make up their minds to see Richmond go,* but must not lose spirit, must not give up. The general left but a few moments ago. My orders are to be in marching order, to lose no time, to begin my preparations to-morrow. These instructions apply to army headquarters only. The army will retain its position *still a time longer,* but the general-in-chief may soon bid it a temporary adieu and repair to another scene of excitement.

EDGE HILL, *February* 24, 1865.

Now that General Johnston has been placed in command of his old army by General Lee, it is not probable that the latter will go to South Carolina—at any rate not immediately. . . . It is not to be denied that our condition at this time is a critical one; but, although it is a crisis in our affairs, it is the same with the enemy. Suppose we were to concentrate on Sherman and crush him, would not the aspect of affairs be entirely changed? Well, *that* is not beyond the range of possibility. Much depends on the check given to Sherman's career. Richmond may be lost to us—*and* Sherman may be overwhelmed. The defeat of Sherman would restore Richmond. To be rid of him would more than compensate for such temporary sacrifice. The rumors in Richmond are great exaggerations of facts. Some of our weaker men have deserted their colors, but the desertion is not so great as reported. We are getting something to eat, and most of our brave fellows are in good heart, although grieved to hear of despondency behind them. All at home should send words of cheer and encouragement to the army.

EDGE HILL, *March* 5, 1865.

I do not, cannot, yet despair; but it is evident that there has been a rapid, radical change in the tone of public sentiment, in which some of our officials participate. Some high in authority tell us that the people are tired, that they are not supported by the people, and that public sentiment has undergone a change. Claiming to be prompted by a desire to prevent the further effusion of blood, these talk of *terms* and *reconstruction*. I do not think our military situation hopeless by any means; but I confess matters are far worse than I ever expected to see them.

EDGE HILL, *March* 23, 1865.

The dread contingency of which some intimation has been given is near at hand. No one can say what the *next week* may bring forth, although the calamity may be deferred a while longer. Now is the hour when we must show of what stuff we are made. It would be worse than useless to indulge in repinings and regrets, which could only impair our efficiency and tend to dishearten those who look to us for protection.

EDGE HILL, *March* 27, 1865.

Matters have not improved since the 23d; there is no cause for hope now which did not exist then. The probable contingency is a foregone conclusion. There appears to be an unaccountable apathy and listlessness in high places. It would be better to face the misfortune bravely, and prepare for it in anticipation. There seems to be no preparation for the removal of the several departments of the government; when the pressure is upon us it may be impracticable. I say nothing of our fight; it was gallantly done, as far as it went. [Allusion is here made to the attack made on the Federal lines by a portion of Gordon's command.]

It is a very simple matter to trace, through the dates here given, the steady progress toward the inevitable doom which, sooner or later, awaited the Confederates in their inflexible purpose to hold the city of Richmond.

General Lee was opposed to that policy which designated certain points as indispensable to be held, except so far and so long as they possessed strategic value to the armies operating in the field. He maintained that the determination to retain possession of such, under all circumstances and at any cost, caused a fallacious value to attach to success in such endeavor, and, in event of failure, entailed a moral loss on us, and assured an elation to the enemy altogether disproportionate to the material benefit to be derived from continued possession; not that he would not have made an earnest effort to save such points as Vicksburg and Richmond from falling into the hands of the enemy —especially the latter, which had a real value, strategically considered ; but when it came to a siege, to settle down behind intrenchments and permit the gradual and complete circumvallation of the place besieged, by an adversary with unlimited resources of men and material, he preferred to move out, to manœuvre, to concentrate, and to fight.

His policy at Petersburg would have been to unite the greater portion of his army — before it wasted away from incessant battle and from desertion[1]—with that under

_____
[1] A few words in regard to this desertion: The condition of affairs through-

General Johnston, and to fall upon General Sherman with the hope of destroying him, and then, with the united armies, to return to confront General Grant. Having the interior line, he could move to accomplish such purpose much more quickly than his adversary could to thwart it. Such a policy involved the giving up of Richmond, it is true; but that which was pursued involved the same thing with a certainty more absolute, and left Sherman to overwhelm Johnston, and at the same time to destroy the granaries of the Confederacy, from which Lee's army was supplied.

In my opinion, as a general rule, the Administration was in perfect accord with General Lee in all his designs, and gave a hearty coöperation in all his movements; but I think the exception was furnished in the persistent effort to hold Richmond and Petersburg, after it became evident that it could be but a question of time, and would probably involve the complete exhaustion of the principal army of the Confederacy.

If it shall be the verdict of posterity that General Lee in any respect fell short of perfection as a military leader, it may perhaps be claimed: first, that he was too careful of the personal feelings of his subordinate commanders, too fearful of wounding their pride, and too solicitous for their reputation. Probably it was this that caused him sometimes to continue in command those of whose fitness for their position he was not convinced, and often led him, either avowedly or tacitly, to assume responsibility for mishaps

out the South at that period was truly deplorable. Hundreds of letters addressed to soldiers were intercepted and sent to army headquarters, in which mothers, wives, and sisters, told of their inability to respond to the appeals of hungry children for bread, or to provide proper care and remedies for the sick; and, in the name of all that was dear, appealed to the men to come home and rescue them from the ills which they suffered and the starvation which threatened them. Surely never was devotion to one's country and to one's duty more sorely tested than was the case with the soldiers of Lee's army during the last year of the war.

clearly attributable to the inefficiency, neglect, or careless-
ness, of others. I have heard him express the wish that
General A had the command of a certain division instead
of General B, when General A was a brigadier in Major-
General B's division, and a recommendation from the
general to the department would doubtless have procured
the change. The world already knows how prone he was
at all times to take upon his own shoulders the responsibility for failure or mishap, and thus shield those from
censure who had really failed to execute his orders or
designs.

In the next place it may be said that he was too law-
abiding, too subordinate to his superiors in civil authority
—those who managed the governmental machinery. Brought
up in the school of the soldier he had early imbibed the
idea that discipline was essential in the military life, and
that subordination was the key-stone of discipline. Obedience to orders was, in his judgment, the cardinal principle
with all good soldiers of every grade. As a rule, no one
can deny the correctness of this view ; but those were extraordinary times, and, in some matters, ordinary rules were
extraordinary evils. General Lee should have been supreme
in all matters touching the movements and discipline of his
army, whereas, under the law and the regulations of the
Department of War made in conformity thereto, he had not
even the power to confer promotion on the field of battle,
and thus to recognize and reward meritorious conduct; and
in matters concerning the movements of his army he was of
course under authority, and more or less controlled by political considerations. Perhaps it could not be otherwise under
our peculiar form of government, but it would never be possible to get the full measure of a man's capacity for military
affairs who was thus trammeled.

A month or two before the close of the war the scope
of General Lee's authority was enlarged, and he was made
general-in-chief of all the armies of the Confederacy; but

the end was then near at hand, and the affairs of the South hopeless.

The traits of character alluded to, excessive generosity and perfect subordination, while they adorned the life of General Lee, are not compatible with the generally accepted notions of perfection in a revolutionary leader.

CHAPTER XII.

On the first day of April General Grant directed a heavy movement against the Confederate right near Five Forks; this necessitated the concentration of every available man at that point to resist the Federal advance, and a consequent stretching out of our line, already so sadly attenuated that at some places it consisted of but one man to every seven yards—nothing more than a skirmish-line. It was without serious resistance, therefore, that on the 2d of April the Federals obtained possession of a portion of the lines between Hatcher's Run and the city. Indeed, we had so few men to contest the matter with them that they were within our lines before it was reported to General Lee or General Hill. From the point occupied by these officers, detached squads of men were observed advancing toward us in the plateau beyond; it was impossible to say whether they were our men or the enemy; and it was for the purpose of solving this doubt and ascertaining the actual condition of affairs in that locality, that General A. P. Hill rode toward these detachments, by the fire from one of which he was shot dead from his horse.

Under cover of a heavy fire of artillery the Federal army now made a general advance. It was apparent that our position could be no longer maintained. General Lee communicated to the authorities at Richmond his intention of evacuating his lines that night, for which emergency they should have been prepared.

During the whole day he was engaged in issuing orders and sending dispatches by couriers and by telegraph, in preparation for this event. Early in the forenoon, while the telegraph-operator was working his instrument at headquarters, under the supervision of the staff-officer charged with the duty of transmitting these orders, a shell came crashing through the house, and the operator declared himself unable longer to work his instrument. He was ordered to detach it, and as the staff-officer and the operator emerged from the house, they with difficulty escaped capture at the hands of the Federal infantry, which just then advanced upon and drove away the battery of artillery which had been placed in position around the house to assist in delaying the advance of the enemy. The comfortable dwelling of Mr. Turnbull, occupied by General Lee as his headquarters, and thus hastily evacuated by the rear-guard of his military family, was soon enveloped in flames. It is to be hoped that the fire was accidental; by General Lee it was then thought and feared to have been by design. One of the many arguments always advanced by him why he should not occupy a house was, that, in event of its falling into the hands of the enemy, the very fact of its having been occupied by him might possibly cause its destruction; and, as before stated, it was only during the last year of the war, when his health was somewhat impaired, that one of his staff had the temerity, on the occasion of one of the general's visits to Richmond, to turn in his tent to the quartermaster's department, and move his effects into a house, which he was thus almost compelled to occupy.

After a gallant resistance our forces were retired to the second or inner line of defense around the city of Petersburg, and there maintained their ground till nightfall. By the dawn of day next morning the lines had been evacuated, and the gallant but sadly-reduced Army of Northern Virginia had made good way in its retreat westwardly toward Amelia Court-House. The intention was to take the direction of Danville, and turn to our advantage the good line for resistance offered by the Dan and Staunton Rivers. The activity of the Federal cavalry and the want of supplies compelled a different course, and the retreat was continued up the South Side Railroad toward Lynchburg.

Despite the great numerical superiority of the Federals and their immense resources, General Lee managed to check their pursuit from time to time, and to continue his retreat for seven days, until, on the morning of the 9th of April, our advance under General Gordon was confronted by the enemy in the neighborhood of Appomattox Court-House. The returns from the various commands made that morning showed an aggregate of eight thousand muskets in line of battle.

On the previous evening I became separated from General Lee in the execution of his orders in regard to the parking of our trains in places of safety, and did not rejoin him until the morning of the 9th. After making my report the general said to me,[1] " Well, colonel, what are we to do ? "

In reply, a fear was expressed that it would be necessary to abandon the trains, which had already occasioned us such great embarrassment ; and the hope was indulged that, relieved of this burden, the army could make good its escape.

" Yes," said the general, " perhaps we could ; but I have had a conference with these gentlemen around me, and they agree that the time has come for capitulation."

" Well, sir," I said, " I can only speak for myself ; to me any other fate is preferable—"

" Such is my individual way of thinking," interrupted the general.

---

[1] General Lee frequently thus addressed those around him—not that he attached any importance to or expected any aid from what might be said in reply ; but, in giving expression to that which occupied his own mind—thinking aloud, so to speak—he at the same time drew from others such information as they might possess, or such views as they might entertain.

"But," I immediately added, "of course, general, it is different with you. You have to think of these brave men and decide not only for yourself, but for them."

"Yes," he replied; "it would be useless and therefore cruel to provoke the further effusion of blood, and I have arranged to meet General Grant with a view to surrender, and wish you to accompany me."

Shortly after this the general, accompanied by Colonel Marshall and myself, started back in the direction from which we had come, to meet General Grant as had been arranged.

We continued some distance without meeting any one after passing our lines; but finally came upon a staff-officer sent by General Grant's order to say to General Lee that he had been prevented from meeting him at that point, and to request that he would meet him upon the other road. General Lee then retraced his steps, and, proceeding toward our front in the direction of Appomattox Court-House, dismounted at a convenient place to await General Grant's communication. Very soon a Federal officer, accompanied by one of General Gordon's staff, rode up to where General Lee was seated in a small orchard on the road-side. This proved to be General Forsythe, of General Sheridan's staff, who was sent by General Sheridan to say that, as he had doubt as to his authority to recognize the informal truce which had been agreed upon between General Gordon and himself, he desired to communicate with General Meade on the subject, and wished permission to pass through our lines as the shortest route. I was assigned to the duty of escorting General Forsythe through our lines and back. This was scarcely accomplished, when General Babcock rode up and announced to General Lee that General Grant was prepared to meet him at the front.

I shrank from this interview, and while I could not then, and cannot now, justify my conduct, I availed myself of the excuse of having taken the two rides through the extent of our lines and to those of the enemy, already mentioned, and did not accompany my chief in this trying ordeal.

The scene witnessed upon the return of General Lee was one certain to impress itself indelibly upon the memory; it can be vividly recalled now, after the lapse of many years, but no description can do it justice.   The men crowded around him, eager to shake him by the hand ; eyes that had been so often illumined with the fire of patriotism and true courage, that had so often glared with defiance in the heat and fury of battle, and so often kindled with enthusiasm and pride in the hour of success, moistened now ; cheeks bronzed by exposure in many campaigns, and withal begrimed with powder and dust, now blanched from deep emotion and suffered the silent tear; tongues that had so often carried dismay to the hearts of the enemy in that indescribable cheer which accompanied " the charge," or that had so often made the air to resound with the pæan of victory, refused utterance now; brave hearts failed that had never quailed in the presence of an enemy ; but the firm and silent pressure of the hand told most eloquently of souls filled with admiration, love, and tender sympathy, for their beloved chief.   He essayed to thank them, but too full a heart paralyzed his speech; he soon sought a short respite from these trying scenes and retired to his private quarters, that he might, in solitude and quiet, commune with his own brave heart and be still.   Thus terminated the career of the Army of Northern Virginia—an army that was never vanquished ; but that, in obedience to the orders of its trusted commander, who was himself yielding obedience to the dictates of a pure and lofty sense of duty to his men and those dependent on them, laid down its arms, and furled the standards never lowered in defeat.

The work of paroling the army was now proceeded with, and was completed on the 10th of April.   On the same day General Meade called to pay his respects to General Lee. The latter reported to his staff, after the visit, that the conversation had naturally turned upon recent events, and that General Meade had asked him how many men he had at Petersburg at the time of General Grant's final assault. He told him in reply that by the last returns he had thirty-three thousand muskets. (In his recital of the matter he appealed to me to know if his memory was correct, and was answered in the affirmative.) General Meade then said, "You mean that you had thirty-three thousand men in the lines immediately around Petersburg?" to which General Lee replied "No," that he had but that number from his left on the Chickahominy River to his right at Dinwiddie Court-House. At this General Meade expressed great surprise, and stated that he then had with him, in the one wing of the Federal army which he commanded, over fifty thousand men.

The number of men and officers paroled, including the stragglers who had caught up with the army, and all the extra-duty or detailed men of every description, was in round numbers between twenty-six and twenty-seven thousand.

On his way to Richmond General Lee stopped for the night near the residence of his brother, Mr. Carter Lee, of Powhatan County; and, although importuned by his brother to pass the night under his roof, the general persisted in pitching his tent by the side of the road, and going into camp as usual. This continued self-denial can only be explained upon the hypothesis that he desired to have his men know that he shared their privations to the very last.

On the 12th day of April he returned to the city of Richmond a paroled prisoner of war, but a monarch still in the hearts of his countrymen, and an object of admiration in the eyes of the civilized world.

CHAPTER XIII.

In June of the same year a United States grand-jury in Norfolk, Virginia, indicted Mr. Davis, General Lee, and others, for treason, or something similar to it. I immediately informed General Lee of the fact, and at the same time expressed a regret that some of our young men were discouraged at not being able to obtain employment, and many in consequence talked of migrating to other countries. He replied as follows:

RICHMOND, VA., *June 17*, 1865.

MY DEAR COLONEL: I am very much obliged to you for your letter of the 13th. I had heard of the indictment by the grand-jury at Norfolk, and made up my mind to let the authorities take their course. I have no wish to avoid any trial the Government may order, and cannot flee. I hope others may be unmolested, and that you at least may be undisturbed.

I am sorry to hear that our returned soldiers· cannot obtain employment. Tell them they must all set to work, and, if they cannot do what they prefer, do what they can. Virginia wants all their aid, all their support, and the presence of all her sons to sustain and recuperate her. They must therefore put themselves in a position to take part in her government, and not be deterred by obstacles in their way. There is much to be done which they only can do. . . .

Very truly yours,   R. E. LEE.

Colonel W. H. TAYLOR.

This letter utterly refutes the charge repeatedly made by writers at the North that, after the cessation of hostilities, General Lee held himself aloof in sullen silence, declining to accept the situation. But two months had elapsed since the surrender at Appomattox—not a sufficient time for the subsidence of the passion engendered by war and the healing of the wounds occasioned by defeat; the hearts of the people of the South were yet filled with resentment and bitter hatred toward their Northern adversaries—and yet he, their greatest captain, counseled a prompt and ready acquiescence in the inevitable, urging his countrymen not to be deterred by seeming obstacles from resuming their citizenship with all its obligations—that is, not to flinch from a compliance with distasteful requirements, but to conform to all legal enactments necessary to enable them to resume the reins of the government of their State, and thus save her from adventurous aliens, and consequent spoliation and ruin.

Soon after this, General Lee conceived the idea of preparing the data for a complete history of the campaigns of the Army of Northern Virginia. Early in August I received the following letter from him, which fully explains his purpose in this regard:

NEAR CARTERSVILLE, *July* 31, 1865.

MY DEAR COLONEL: I am desirous that the bravery and devotion of the Army of Northern Virginia shall be correctly transmitted to posterity. This is the only tribute that can now be paid to the worth of its noble officers and soldiers; and I am anxious to collect the necessary data for the history of the campaigns in Virginia, from the commencement of its organization to its final surrender. I am particularly anxious that its actual strength in the different battles it has fought be correctly stated. You know all its official returns, records, etc., from the time of my connection with it, have been lost or destroyed.

As you prepared the tri-monthly returns for so long, and tested their accuracy, I have thought its gradual changes may have been impressed upon your memory, and that you might state with some confidence its effective strength, at each of the great battles it has fought, in infantry, cavalry, and artillery. You may also have some memoranda within your reach that would assist your memory.   Please give me at least the benefit of your recollection. . . .

Very truly yours,   R. E. LEE.

Colonel WALTER H. TAYLOR.

Upon the receipt of this letter, I communicated with Mr. Thomas White, of Alexandria, Virginia, a detailed soldier and most estimable gentleman, who occupied, during the period of the whole war, the position of chief clerk in the office of the adjutant-general of the Army of Northern Virginia, and whose duty it was, under the supervision of the adjutant-general, to compile the army field-returns from those of the several corps, and requested him to give his recollection of our effective strength at the important periods of the war. In response to this request, Mr. White sent the following statement of the effective strength of the army at the several dates given, according to his recollection :

SEVEN DAYS' BATTLES AROUND RICHMOND.

Effective infantry	73,000
Effective cavalry	3,000
Effective artillery	4,000
Total effective of all arms	80,000

CEDAR RUN, OR SLAUGHTER'S MOUNTAIN.

Effective infantry	18,500
Effective cavalry	2,000
Effective artillery	1,000
Total effective of all arms	21,500

SECOND MANASSAS.

Effective infantry	38,000
Effective cavalry	5,000
Effective artillery	4,000
Total effective of all arms	47,000

HARPER'S FERRY.

Jackson	12,000
J. G. Walker	3,000
Infantry	**15,000**

CRAMPTON GAP.

McLaws	4,000
Anderson	4,000
Infantry	**8,000**

BOONSBORO'.

Longstreet	8,000
D. H. Hill	7,000
Infantry	**15,000**

SHARPSBURG.

Effective infantry	33,000
Effective cavalry	4,500
Effective artillery	4,000
Total effective of all arms	**41,500**

FREDERICKSBURG.

Effective infantry	50,500
Effective cavalry	4,000
Effective artillery	4,000
Total effective of all arms	**58,500**

CHANCELLORSVILLE.

Effective infantry	42,000
Effective cavalry	4,000
Effective artillery	3,000
Total effective of all arms	**49,000**

GETTYSBURG.

Effective infantry	55,000
Effective cavalry	7,000
Effective artillery	5,000
Total effective of all arms	**67,000**

BRISTOE STATION.

```
Effective infantry........................................  32,000
Effective cavalry.........................................   6,000
Effective artillery.......................................   4,500
                                                           --------
     Total effective of all arms.........................  42,500
```

MINE RUN.

```
Effective infantry........................................  30,500
Effective cavalry.........................................   6,000
Effective artillery.......................................   4,500
                                                           --------
     Total effective of all arms.........................  41,000
```

WILDERNESS.

```
Effective infantry........................................  48,500
Effective cavalry.........................................   8,000
Effective artillery.......................................   5,000
                                                           --------
     Total effective of all arms.........................  61,500
```

SPOTTSYLVANIA COURT-HOUSE.

```
Effective infantry........................................  41,500
Effective cavalry.........................................   7,000
Effective artillery.......................................   4,500
                                                           --------
     Total effective of all arms.........................  53,000
```

COLD HARBOR.

```
Effective infantry........................................  47,000
Effective cavalry.........................................   6,000
Effective artillery.......................................   4,500
                                                           --------
     Total effective of all arms.........................  57,500
```

PETERSBURG, JUNE 21, 1864.

```
Effective infantry........................................  36,000
Effective cavalry.........................................   4,000
Effective artillery.......................................   3,500
                                                           --------
     Total effective of all arms.........................  43,500
```

PETERSBURG, OCTOBER 1, 1864.

```
Effective infantry........................................  32,000
Effective cavalry.........................................   3,000
Effective artillery.......................................   3,500
                                                           --------
     Total effective of all arms.........................  38,500
```

PETERSBURG, JANUARY 1, 1865.

Effective infantry.................................... 38,500
Effective cavalry.................................... 2,500
Effective artillery.................................. 4,500
                                                     _____
   Total effective of all arms...................... 45,500

PETERSBURG, APRIL 1, 1865.

Effective infantry.................................... 36,000
Effective cavalry.................................... 3,500
Effective artillery.................................. 4,000
                                                     _____
   Total effective of all arms...................... 43,500

A duplicate of the statement of Mr. White was sent by him to General Lee, who, on the 2d of November, 1865, wrote as follows:

LEXINGTON, VA., *November* 2, 1865.

MY DEAR COLONEL: Your letter of August has remained a long time unanswered. Since then, I have received from White, to whom I had written, a statement of our effective strength at the chief battles, which appeared to me larger at some points than I thought. Marshall has also given me his recollection on the subject, which does not entirely correspond with mine, either. When I get yours, I shall have to make a just average.

I have made no progress as yet in writing, and very little in collecting information. Every one, I suppose, is embarrassed by loss of papers, and the necessary devotion to his business. It is as much as I can do to answer applications of our distressed soldiers and bereaved parents. Matters are working much smoother, and time will cure all things.

                  Most truly yours,   R. E. LEE.

Colonel WALTER H. TAYLOR.

The reader will observe that, with the statement of Mr. White before him, General Lee's only criticism in regard thereto was, that it represented our strength to have been *greater at certain periods than he thought it was.* It is very much to be regretted that the general did not prepare, over

his own signature, a statement of the effective strength of
his army at the most important epochs in its history.   Such
a statement would have been accepted without question by
the world.   In its absence, his letter commenting upon the
foregoing statement—which fortunately has been preserved
—assumes great historical value, for it establishes beyond
all cavil or doubt the extent of the disparity of numbers between the two armies, should Mr. White's estimates be made
the standard of comparison.

CHAPTER XIV.

The Strength of the Army of Northern Virginia, taken from the Original Returns now on File in the Archive-Office of the War Department, Washington, D. C.

AFTER the notes contained in the preceding chapter had been prepared, and when I was about to address myself to the task of reproducing the statement of the strength of the Army of Northern Virginia, made by me from memory, soon after the war, in compliance with the request of General Lee, I ascertained that some of the field and monthly returns of that army were on file in the archives of the War Department at Washington.

Inasmuch as several unsuccessful attempts had been made to obtain permission to examine the Confederate papers there on file, and recognizing the force of the objection of the officials in charge to a general inspection of those documents, it was with considerable misgiving, and indeed with but little hope, that I caused application in my behalf to be made to the authorities for permission to examine the army returns alluded to; relying solely upon the fact of my having supervised the preparation of those returns for several years as an argument in favor of having an exception made in my case.

Success crowned my effort, and I take this opportunity of expressing my appreciation of the very kind and courteous treatment I received at the hands of the officials of the War Department, who extended to me every facility for the accomplishment of my purpose; and at the same time I take pleasure in assuring my former comrades-in-arms of the evident purpose of the Government authorities charged with the custody of these records to discard all sectional bias in the prosecution of their labors, and to preserve faithfully and impartially all documents which are now in their custody, or which may be hereafter committed to their care, in order that, so far as it is in their power, the truth, and nothing but the truth, shall be preserved. Let us indulge the hope that the day is not far distant when the American people, without distinction, will find pleasure in the contemplation of all that was manly, all that was virtuous, all that was noble, all that was praiseworthy, in the recent struggle between the sections, whether developed on the side of the North or that of the South; and that the next generation will cherish, with pardonable pride, the remembrance of the deeds of valor, sacrifice, and noble daring, with which the history of that war so richly abounds, whether the heroes thereof wore the blue or the gray.

Let censure fall only where fanatics feigned to be patriots, or men forgot their manhood, and, screened behind an alleged military necessity, gave evidence of an evil heart in deeds of malignant cruelty or wanton destruction; and let merit be acknowledged and praise be bestowed *wherever* firm devotion to principle and to duty found illustration in deeds of valor and of sacrifice.

As soon as practicable I availed myself of the permission accorded me, and proceeded to make an examination of the army returns on file in the Department. The first paper that was examined by me proved to be an informal return of the strength of the army commanded by General Joseph E. Johnston, which I at once recognized as having been on file in General Lee's office, and the indorsement upon which was in my own handwriting, except the date, which was added either by Mr. Davis or General Long, who was then private secretary to General Lee, and read as follows: " Army near Richmond, Department of Northern Virginia, May 21, 1862." Within was the following statement of the strength of the several commands of which that army was then composed:

FIRST DIVISION—MAJOR-GENERAL G. W. SMITH.

Whiting's brigade....................................	2,398
Hood's brigade.....................................	1,922
W. H. Hampton's brigade...........................	2,225
S. R. Hatton's brigade...............................	2,030
Pettigrew's brigade..................................	2,017
Total...	10,592

SECOND DIVISION—MAJOR-GENERAL LONGSTREET.

A. P. Hill's brigade..................................	2,512
Pickett's brigade....................................	2,460
R. H. Anderson's brigade............................	2,168
Wilcox's brigade....................................	2,616
Colston's brigade...................................	1,750
Pryor's brigade.....................................	2,310.
Total...	13,816

THIRD DIVISION—MAJOR-GENERAL MAGRUDER.

McLaws's brigade...................................	2,084
Kershaw's brigade...................................	2,567
Griffith's brigade....................................	2,534
H. Cobb's brigade...................................	3,796
Toombs's brigade	2,357
D. R. Jones's brigade................................	2,342
Reserve artillery—Cabell............................	240
Total...	15,920

FOURTH DIVISION—MAJOR-GENERAL D. H. HILL.

Early's brigade.....................................	2,380
Rodes's brigade.....................................	3,040
Colonel Ward's command............................	890
Raines's brigade....................................	1,830
Featherstone's brigade...............................	2,224
Colonel Crump's command...........................	787
Total...	11,151

Cavalry brigade.....................................	1,289
Reserve artillery :	
Pendleton's	611
Washington.......................................	309
Total...	920
Total strength of all arms.........................	53,688

I then examined carefully all the field and monthly returns of the "Department of Northern Virginia" on file in the Archive-Office, and copied therefrom the following extracts, which make an authoritative statement of the strength of the army commanded by General Lee at the periods named :

DATE OF RETURN, JULY 20, 1862.

DEPARTMENT OF NORTHERN VIRGINIA AND NORTH CAROLINA.	PRESENT FOR DUTY.	
	Officers.	Enlisted Men.
Department of North Carolina.....................	722	11,509
Longstreet's division............................	557	7,929
D. H. Hill's division............................	550	8,998
McLaws's division................................	514	7,188
A. P. Hill's division............................	519	10,104
Anderson's division..............................	357	5,760
D. R. Jones's division...........................	213	3,500
Whiting's division...............................	252	3,600
Stuart's cavalry.................................	295	3,740
Pendleton's artillery............................	103	1,716
Rhett's artillery................................	78	1,355
Total, including Department of North Carolina..	4,160	65,399

SEPTEMBER 22, 1862.

ARMY OF NORTHERN VIRGINIA.	PRESENT FOR DUTY.	
	Officers.	Enlisted Men.
Longstreet's command............................	1,410	19,001
Jackson's command:		
D. H. Hill's division.........................	310	4,739
A. P. Hill's division.........................	318	4,435
Ewell's division..............................	280	3,144
Jackson's division............................	183	2,367
Total	2,501	33,686

SEPTEMBER 30, 1862.

ARMY OF NORTHERN VIRGINIA.	PRESENT FOR DUTY.	
	Officers.	Enlisted Men.
Longstreet's command............................	1,927	26,489
Jackson's command...............................	1,699	21,728
Reserve artillery...............................	50	716
Total	3,676	48,933
No report of cavalry.		

OCTOBER 10, 1862.

ARMY OF NORTHERN VIRGINIA.	PRESENT FOR DUTY.	
	Officers.	Enlisted Men.
Longstreet's command...........................	2,022	27,934
Jackson's command..............................	1,841	25,603
Cavalry	395	5,338
Reserve artillery..............................	48	858
Total	4,306	59,733

NEAR WINCHESTER, OCTOBER 20, 1862.

ARMY OF NORTHERN VIRGINIA.	PRESENT FOR DUTY.	
	Officers.	Enlisted Men.
Longstreet's command...........................	2,241	29,748
Jackson's command..............................	2,002	26,368
Cavalry.......................................	417	6,119
Reserve artillery..............................	45	865
Total.....................................	4,705	63,100

CULPEPER COURT-HOUSE, NOVEMBER 10, 1862.

ARMY OF NORTHERN VIRGINIA.	PRESENT FOR DUTY.	
	Officers.	Enlisted Men.
Longstreet's command...........................	2,308	29,522
Jackson's command..............................	2,243	29,461
Cavalry.......................................	457	6,697
Reserve artillery..............................	No report.	No report.
Total.....................................	5,008	65,680

FREDERICKSBURG, NOVEMBER 20, 1862.

ARMY OF NORTHERN VIRGINIA.	PRESENT FOR DUTY.	
	Officers.	Enlisted Men.
Longstreet's command...........................	2,325	29,288
Jackson's command..............................	2,346	30,441
Cavalry.......................................	603	8,551
Reserve artillery..............................	No report.	No report.
Total.....................................	5,274	68,280

FREDERICKSBURG, DECEMBER 10, 1862.

ARMY OF NORTHERN VIRGINIA.	PRESENT FOR DUTY.	
	Officers.	Enlisted Men.
Longstreet's command:		
Anderson's division...........................	531	7,083
McLaws's division.............................	559	7,311
Pickett's division.............................	675	6,860
Hood's division...............................	521	6,795
Ransom's division.............................	253	3,595
Alexander's artillery..........................	24	402
Walton's artillery.............................	13	184
Total under Longstreet.................	2,576	32,230
Jackson's command:		
Jackson's division............................	463	4,526
D. H. Hill's division..........................	588	8,327
Ewell's division..............................	594	7,100
A. P. Hill's division..........................	781	10,743
Brown's artillery.............................	24	449
Total under Jackson...................	2,450	31,145
Cavalry......................................	602	8,512
Reserve artillery..............................	36	677
Total.................................	5,664	72,564

FREDERICKSBURG, DECEMBER 20, 1862.

ARMY OF NORTHERN VIRGINIA.	PRESENT FOR DUTY.	
	Officers.	Enlisted Men.
Longstreet's command...........................	2,620	31,670
Jackson's command.............................	2,353	29,046
Cavalry (report of December 10th used).............	602	8,512
Reserve artillery...............................	38	683
Total......................................	5,613	69,911

FREDERICKSBURG, DECEMBER 31, 1862.

Longstreet's command—Total effective....................	30,060
Jackson's " "	27,608
Cavalry " "	8,814
Artillery " "	4,490
Total effective of all arms.........................	70,972

FREDERICKSBURG, JANUARY 31, 1863.

Longstreet's command—Total effective....................	28,696
Jackson's " "	29,698
Cavalry "	7,125
Artillery "	2,874
Valley District (General W. E. Jones).....................	3,833

Total effective, including troops in the Valley of Virginia 72,226

FREDERICKSBURG, FEBRUARY 28, 1863.

Anderson's and McLaws's divisions—Total effective.........	14,540
Jackson's command "	30,977
Cavalry "	5,912
Artillery "	3,552
Valley District "	3,578

Total effective, including troops in the Valley of Virginia 58,559

FREDERICKSBURG, MARCH 31, 1863.

Anderson's and McLaws's divisions [1] —Total effective.......	15,649
Jackson's four divisions "	33,333
Cavalry "	6,509
Artillery in rear "	1,621
Valley District "	3,186

Total effective, including troops in the Valley of Virginia 60,298

FREDERICKSBURG, MAY 20, 1863.

ARMY OF NORTHERN VIRGINIA.	PRESENT FOR DUTY.	
	Officers.	Enlisted Men.
Longstreet's command :		
Anderson's division...........................	553	6,439
McLaw's division..............................	579	6,454
Pickett's division.............................	558	5,847
Hood's division...............................	640	6,858
Total under Longstreet..................	2,330	25,598
Hill's command :		
Hill's division................................	722	7,986
Rodes's division...............................	545	6,457
Early's division...............................	496	5,925
Johnson's division.............................	419	4,783
Total under Hill......................	2,182	25,151
Cavalry (one regiment not reported)	482	6,524
Artillery (Dearing's battalion and two batteries not re-ported).................................	245	4,708
Total................................	5,239	61,981

[1] Pickett, Hood, and Ransom, detached.

FREDERICKSBURG, MAY 31, 1863.

Longstreet's command—Total effective.................... 26,583
A. P. Hill's   "   "   27,773
Cavalry   "   9,536
Artillery   "   4,460

Total effective of all arms......................... 68,352

BUNKER HILL, JULY 20, 1863.

ARMY OF NORTHERN VIRGINIA.	PRESENT FOR DUTY.	
	Officers.	Enlisted Men.
Longstreet's Corps: McLaws's division, Pickett's division, Hood's division	1,186	11,731
Ewell's Corps: Rodes's division, Early's division, Johnson's division	1,277	12,440
Hill's Corps: Anderson's division, Heth's division, Pender's division	961	8,930
Cavalry..	No report.	No report.
Artillery..	274	4,589
Total..	3,698	37,690

CULPEPER COURT-HOUSE, JULY 31, 1863.

Longstreet's corps—Total effective........................ 12,823
Ewell's corps   "   12,369
Hill's corps   "   11,207
Artillery corps   "   4,736
Cavalry corps.................................. No report.

Total effective of all arms......................... 41,135

ORANGE COURT-HOUSE, AUGUST 10, 1863.

ARMY OF NORTHERN VIRGINIA.	PRESENT FOR DUTY.	
	Officers.	Enlisted Men.
Longstreet's corps................................	1,279	13,559
Ewell's corps.....................................	1,371	14,422
Hill's corps......................................	1,115	12,398
Cavalry corps.....................................	595	8,404
Artillery corps...................................	277	4,880
Total..	4,637	53,663

ORANGE COURT-HOUSE, AUGUST 20, 1863.

ARMY OF NORTHERN VIRGINIA.	PRESENT FOR DUTY.	
	Officers.	Enlisted Men.
Longstreet's corps.............................	1,242	13,323
Ewell's corps.................................	1,369	14,900
Hill's corps..................................	1,094	13,059
Cavalry corps................................	617	8,094
Artillery corps...............................	290	4,906
Total..................................	4,612	54,282

ORANGE COURT-HOUSE, AUGUST 31, 1863.

Longstreet's corps—Total effective........................... 14,668
Ewell's corps   "   15,428
Hill's corps   "   13,601
Cavalry corps (1,333 dismounted) 7,701
Artillery corps—Total effective........................... 4,929

Total effective of all arms........................... 56,327

ORANGE COURT-HOUSE, SEPTEMBER 10, 1863.

ARMY OF NORTHERN VIRGINIA.	PRESENT FOR DUTY.	
	Officers.	Enlisted Men.
Ewell's corps.................................	1,274	15,804
Hill's corps..................................	1,034	14,087
Cooke's brigade (unattached)....................	134	2,100
Artillery....................................	147	3,226
Cavalry.....................................	No report.	No report.
Total..................................	2,589	35,217

Longstreet's corps detached.

ORANGE COURT-HOUSE, SEPTEMBER 20, 1863.

ARMY OF NORTHERN VIRGINIA.	PRESENT FOR DUTY.	
	Officers.	Enlisted Men.
Ewell's corps.................................	1,391	16,235
Hill's corps..................................	1,075	14,297
Cooke's brigade...............................	135	2,045
Cavalry corps................................	560	7,547
Artillery corps...............................	184	3,337
Total..................................	3,345	43,461

ORANGE COURT-HOUSE, SEPTEMBER 30, 1863.

```
Ewell's  corps — Total effective.........................  16,638
Hill's corps              "       ....................  .....  15,073
Cooke's brigade           "       .........................   2,150
Cavalry corps             "       .........................   6,744
Artillery corps           "       .........................   3,762
```
                                                            _____
```
    Total effective of all arms.........................  44,367
```

NEAR BRANDY STATION, OCTOBER 20, 1863.

ARMY OF NORTHERN VIRGINIA.	PRESENT FOR DUTY.	
	Officers.	Enlisted Men.
Ewell's corps....................................	1,526	16,595
Hill's corps....................................	1,328	16,069
Cavalry corps....................................	505	6,867
Artillery corps....................................	218	3,620
Total	3,577	43,151

Cooke's brigade attached to Heth's division.

BRANDY STATION, OCTOBER 31, 1863.

```
Ewell's  corps — Total effective.........................  17,097
Hill's corps              "       .........................  16,533
Cavalry corps             "       .........................   7,917
Artillery corps           "       .........................   4,067
```
                                                            _____
```
    Total effective of all arms.........................  45,614
```

ORANGE COURT-HOUSE, NOVEMBER 20, 1863.

ARMY OF NORTHERN VIRGINIA.	PRESENT FOR DUTY.	
	Officers.	Enlisted Men.
Ewell's corps....................................	1,321	15,649
Hill's corps....................................	1,361	17,522
Cavalry corps....................................	495	7,139
Artillery corps....................................	233	4,418
Total	3,410	44,728

ORANGE COURT-HOUSE, DECEMBER 10, 1863.

ARMY OF NORTHERN VIRGINIA.	PRESENT FOR DUTY.	
	Officers.	Enlisted Men.
Ewell's corps....................................	1,413	15,447
Hill's corps.....................................	1,415	17,872
Cavalry corps................................	552	7,481
Artillery corps..................................	244	4,371
Provost-guard...................................	18	311
Headquarters battalion...........................	9	114
Total......................................	3,651	45,596
Add Twenty first North Carolina Regiment just reported, not included in above......................	.....	500
Total...................................	3,651	46,096

ORANGE COURT-HOUSE, DECEMBER 20, 1863.

ARMY OF NORTHERN VIRGINIA.	PRESENT FOR DUTY.	
	Officers.	Enlisted Men.
Ewell's corps....................................	1,413	15,735
Hill's corps[1].....................................	1,187	15,543
Cavalry corps....................................	551	7,530
Artillery corps..................................	244	4,371
Headquarters battalion...........................	8	106
Total...................................	3,403	43,285

ORANGE COURT-HOUSE, DECEMBER 31, 1863.

Ewell's corps—Total effective............................	15,540
Hill's corps "	15,468
Cavalry corps "	7,550
Artillery corps "	4,138
Total effective of all arms...........................	42,696
Unattached commands, Valley District, Maryland line, provost guard, and headquarters battalion......................	862

[1] Walker's brigade, Heth's division, and Thomas's brigade, Wilcox's division, detached.

ORANGE COURT-HOUSE, JANUARY 10, 1864.

DEPARTMENT OF NORTHERN VIRGINIA.		PRESENT FOR DUTY.	
		Officers.	Enlisted Men.
Second Corps, Lieutenant-General Ewell.	Early's division..........	406	4,714
	Johnson's division	410	4,476
	Rodes's division	440	6,134
		1,256	15,324
Third Corps, Lieutenant-General Hill.	Anderson's division.......	412	5,957
	Heth's division	258	4,391
	Wilcox's division	325	4,972
		995	15,320
Cavalry Corps, Major-General Stuart.	Hampton's division.......	273	3,931
	Fitz Lee's division	250	3,617
		523	7,548
Artillery corps...............................		217	4,338
Total Army of Northern Virginia............		2,991	42,530
Unattached commands, Maryland line, provost-guard, and headquarters battalion		67	1,073
Total Department of Northern Virginia........		3,058	43,603
Valley District not reported.			

ORANGE COURT-HOUSE, JANUARY 31, 1864.

Total Effective.

Second Corps, Lt.-Gen. Ewell.
{ Early's division.... 3,604 Hoke's brigade detatched.
Johnson's division.. 4,156
Rodes's division ... 5,042 { 12th and 21st Ga., and 43d N. C. Regiments not reported.

12,802

Third Corps, Lt.-Gen. Hill.
{ Anderson's division 5,577
Heth's division.... 4,272 Walker's brigade detached.
Wilcox's division.. 4,896 Thomas's brigade detached.

14,745

Cavalry Corps, Maj.-Gen. Stuart
{ Hampton's division, 2,198
Fitz Lee's........ 1,162
{ Rosser's brigade, Lee's brigade, three regiments of Wickham's brigade, and two of Gordon's, not reported.

3,360

Unattach'd Commands.
{ Artillery corps............... 3,842
Maryland line............... 706
Provost-guard............... 281
Headquarters battalion....... 113

Total effective.............. 35,849

ORANGE COURT-HOUSE, FEBRUARY 10, 1864.

ARMY OF NORTHERN VIRGINIA.		PRESENT FOR DUTY.	
		Officers.	Enlisted Men.
Second Corps, Lieutenant-General Ewell.	Early's division..........	295	3,653[1]
	Johnson's division.......	364	4,140
	Rodes's division	392	5,129[2]
		1,051	12,922
Third Corps, Lieutenant-General Hill.	Anderson's division......	415	5,595
	Heth's division..........	267	4,411[3]
	Wilcox's division	330	4,962[4]
		1,012	14,968
Cavalry corps..................................		Not	reported.
Artillery (First Corps only).......................		139	2,588
Maryland line..................................		46	706
Provost-guard..................................		17	228
Headquarters battalion...........................		7	123
Total		2,272	31,535

ORANGE COURT-HOUSE, MARCH 10, 1864.

ARMY OF NORTHERN VIRGINIA.		PRESENT FOR DUTY.	
		Officers.	Enlisted Men.
Second Corps, Lieutenant-General Ewell.	Early's division..........	229	3,781[5]
	Johnson's division.......	392	4,362
	Rodes's...............	429	5,898[6]
		1,050	14,041
Third Corps, Lieutenant-General Hill.	Anderson's division......	419	5,684
	Heth's division..........	406	6,038
	Wilcox's division........	440	6,571
		1,265	18,293
Cavalry.....................................		Not	reported.
Artillery corps.................................		200	4,100
Provost-guard and headquarters battalion...........		26	428
Total..................................		2,541	36,862

[1] Hoke's brigade detached.
[2] Twelfth and Twenty-first Georgia and Forty-third North Carolina Regiments detached.
[3] Walker's brigade detached.   [4] Thomas's brigade detached.
[5] Hoke's brigade detached.
[6] Twenty-first Georgia and Forty-third North Carolina Regiments detached.

ORANGE COURT-HOUSE, MARCH 20, 1864.

DEPARTMENT OF NORTHERN VIRGINIA.		PRESENT FOR DUTY.	
		Officers.	Enlisted Men.
Second Corps, Lieutenant-General Ewell.	Early's division..........	310	3,917[1]
	Johnson's division.......	426	4,568
	Rodes's division.........	426	6,143[2]
		1,162	14,628
Third Corps, Lieutenant-General Hill.	Anderson's division.......	452	5,831
	Heth's division..........	419	6,245
	Wilcox's division........	474	6,793
		1,345	18,869
Cavalry corps.................................		292	4,478[3]
Artillery corps...............................		207	4,066
Total Army of Northern Virginia..........		3,006	42,041
Valley District...............................		55	736
Maryland line................................		41	761
Provost-guard................................		20	237
Headquarters battalion........................		12	200
Total Department of Northern Virginia......		3,134	43,975

ORANGE COURT-HOUSE, APRIL 10, 1864.

DEPARTMENT OF NORTHERN VIRGINIA.		PRESENT FOR DUTY.	
		Officers.	Enlisted Men.
Second Corps, Lieutenant-General Ewell.	Early's division..........	349	4,185[4]
	Johnson's division.......	496	4,849
	Rodes's division	502	6,603[5]
		1,347	15,637
Third Corps, Lieutenant-General Hill.	Anderson's division	490	6,381
	Heth's division	460	6,507
	Wilcox's division........	515	7,311
		1,465	20,199

[1] Hoke's brigade detached.
[2] Twenty-first Georgia and Forty-third North Carolina Regiments detached.
[3] Chambliss's and Lomax's brigades not reported.
[4] Hoke's brigade detached.
[5] Twenty-first Georgia and Forty-third North Carolina Regiments detached.

ORANGE COURT-HOUSE, APRIL 10, 1864—*Continued.*

DEPARTMENT OF NORTHERN VIRGINIA.	PRESENT FOR DUTY.	
	Officers.	Enlisted Men.
Cavalry Corps, Major-General Stuart. { Hampton's division......	180	2,667
Fitz Lee's division........	285	4,796
	465	7,463
Artillery corps.................................	234	4,486
Total Army of Northern Virginia.........	3,511	47,785
Valley District.................................	Not	reported.
Maryland line..................................	42	737
Provost-guard.................................	22	286
Headquarters battalion.........................	12	223
Total Department of Northern Virginia....	3,587	49,031

ORANGE COURT-HOUSE, APRIL 20, 1864.

DEPARTMENT OF NORTHERN VIRGINIA.	PRESENT FOR DUTY.	
	Officers.	Enlisted Men.
Second Corps, Lieutenant-General Ewell. { Early's division..........	356	4,182
Johnson's division........	506	4,894
Rodes's division	512	6,629
	1,374	15,705
Third Corps, Lieutenant-General Hill. { Anderson's division......	507	6,439
Heth's division..........	516	6,948
Wilcox's division	528	7,261
	1,551	20,648
Cavalry Corps, Major-General Stuart. { Hampton's division......	286	2,931
Fitz Lee's division........	279	5,001
	565	7,932
Artillery corps	237	4,617
Total Army of Northern Virginia.........	3,727	48,902
Valley District.................................	Not	reported.
Maryland line..................................	45	760
Provost-guard.................................	27	293
Headquarters battalion of couriers................	11	219
Total Department of Northern Virginia....	3,810	50,174

Hoke's brigade, Early's division, and two regiments of Rodes's division, detached.

PETERSBURG, JUNE 30, 1864.

TROOPS UNDER GENERAL LEE.		PRESENT FOR DUTY.	
		Officers.	Enlisted Men.
Depart. N. C. and So. Va., General Beauregard.	{ B. R. Johnson's division ..	472	6,364
	{ Hoke's division..........	350	4,936
		822	11,300
First Corps, Major - General Anderson.	{ Pickett's division	348	4,536
	{ Field's division..........	413	4,344
	{ Kershaw's division.......	337	4,180
		1,098	13,060
Third Corps, Lieutenant- General Hill.	{ Anderson's division	411	4,880
	{ Heth's division..........	440	5,159
	{ Wilcox's division........	351	4,289
		1,202	14,328
Cavalry Corps, Major - General Hampton.	{ Hampton's division.......	...	2,888
	{ Fitz Lee's division	130	1,553
	{ W. H. F. Lee's division...	173	2,677
		303	7,118
Artillery corps................................		257	5,263
Total...............................		3,682	51,069

Second Corps detached under General Early. Dearing's brigade of cavalry not reported. Only three battalions of artillery of the Second Corps reported.

NEAR PETERSBURG, JULY 10, 1864.

TROOPS UNDER GENERAL LEE.		PRESENT FOR DUTY.	
		Officers.	Enlisted Men.
Dept. N. C. and So. Va., General Beauregard.	{ B. R. Johnson's division..	487	6,391
	{ Hoke's division...........	346	4,678
		833	11,069
First Corps, Major-General Anderson.	{ Pickett's division........	381	4,472
	{ Field's division..........	427	4,284
	{ Kershaw's division.......	342	4,217
		1,150	12,973

NEAR PETERSBURG, JULY 10, 1864—*Continued.*

TROOPS UNDER GENERAL LEE.		PRESENT FOR DUTY.	
		Officers.	Enlisted Men.
Third Corps, Lieutenant-General Hill.	Anderson's division......	468	5,567
	Heth's division.........	447	5,276
	Wilcox's division........	373	4,410
		1,288	15,253
Cavalry Corps, Major-General Hampton.	Hampton's division.......	195	2,888
	Fitz Lee's division........	115	1,591
	W. H. F. Lee's division....	216	3,957
		526	8,436
Artillery corps..................................		276	5,293
Total......................................		4,073	53,024

PETERSBURG, AUGUST 31, 1864.

Total Effective.

First Corps, Anderson.	Pickett's division.................	4,544	
	Field's division...................	3,944	
	Kershaw's division...............	3,445	
			11,933
Second Corps, Early.	Breckinridge's division............	2,104	
	Rodes's division..................	3,013	
	Gordon's division.................	2,544	
	Ramseur's division...............	1,909	
			9,570
Third Corps, A. P. Hill.	Mahone's division.................	4,094	
	Heth's division...................	4,075	
	Wilcox's division.................	4,054	
	Fifth Alabama Battalion...........	151	
			12,374
Cavalry Corps.	Hampton's division...............	2,769	
	Fitz Lee's division...............	Detached.	
	W. H. F. Lee's division............	2,575	
	Dearing's brigade.................	1,395	
			6,739
Artillery corps................................			3,631
Total effective of all arms....................			44,247

PETERSBURG, SEPTEMBER 10, 1864.

ARMY OF NORTHERN VIRGINIA.	PRESENT FOR DUTY.	
	Officers.	Enlisted Men.
First Corps, Anderson. { Pickett's division..................	361	4,542
Field's division...................	409	4,046
Kershaw's division................	No report.	....
	770	8,588
Second Corps, Early. { Breckinridge's division.............	194	2,172
Rodes's division..................	307	3,244
Gordon's division.................	271	2,690
Ramseur's division................	182	2,010
Carter's artillery.................	39	818
	993	10,934
Third Corps, A. P. Hill. { Heth's division....................	323	4,159
Mahone's division.................	321	4,120
Wilcox's division..................	351	4,211
Fifth Alabama Battalion...........	14	145
	1,009	12,635
Cavalry Corps, Hampton. { Hampton's division...............	184	2,736
Fitz Lee's division.................	....	Detached.
W. H. F. Lee's division............	133	2,545
Lomax's division.................	353	3,215
Horse artillery...................	16	225
Dearing's brigade.................	82	1,430
	768	10,151
Artillery corps	249	4,486
Total.......................................	3,789	46,794

CHAFIN'S BLUFF, OCTOBER 20, 1864.

ARMY OF NORTHERN VIRGINIA.	PRESENT FOR DUTY.	
	Officers.	Enlisted Men.
First Corps, Longstreet. { Pickett's division...............	364	4,967
Field's division.................	330	3,491
Hoke's division.................	301	3,787
	995	12,245

CHAFIN'S BLUFF, OCTOBER 20, 1864—*Continued.*

ARMY OF NORTHERN VIRGINIA.		PRESENT FOR DUTY.	
		Officers.	Enlisted Men.
Third Corps, A. P. Hill.	Heth's division..................	337	4,540
	Wilcox's division...............	360	4,730
	Mahone's division..............	348	4,368
		1,045	13,638
Cavalry Corps, Hampton.	Hampton's division.............	101	1,330
	W. H. F. Lee's division..........	130	2,834
	Dearing's brigade...............	70	1,211
	Horse artillery..................	3	78
		304	5,453
Artillery corps..................................		252	4,246
First District, Department North Carolina and Southern Virginia, Wise's command..................		149	2,248
Provost-guard.................................		22	194
Total.....................................		2,767	38,024

NOTE.—No return received of the troops serving in the Valley District, nor of Johnson's division, nor of the Second and Third Military Districts of the Department of North Carolina and Southern Virginia. Hoke's division is included in the above report of Longstreet's corps in place of Kershaw's division, detached (in the Valley of Virginia). Of the cavalry, 1,249 men are dismounted.

PETERSBURG, OCTOBER 31, 1864.

			Total Effective.
First Corps, Longstreet.	Pickett's division.............	5,764	
	Field's division...............	3,994	
	Hoke's division...............	4,505	
			14,263
Third Corps, A. P. Hill.	Heth's division...............	4,198	
	Wilcox's division.............	5,034	
	Mahone's division............	4,546	
			13,778
B. R. Johnson's division........................			6,329
Cavalry Corps, Hampton.	Hampton's division...........	1,435	
	W. H. F. Lee's division........	2,888	
	Dearing's brigade.............	1,248	
	Horse artillery...............	83	
			5,654
Artillery corps			5,057
Total effective of all arms, Army of Northern Virginia,			45,081

Total Effective.

Total effective of all arms, Army of Northern Virginia,   45,081

First Military District, Department of North Carolina
    and Southern Virginia, Wise commanding.......   2,226

Third Military District, Department of North Carolina
    and Southern Virginia, Whiting commanding....   3,863

Early's command in the Valley of Virginia.	Rodes's division...............	2,316
	Early's division...............	1,794
	Gordon's division.............	2,073
	Wharton's division...........	1,538
	Kershaw's division...........	2,856
	Artillery....................	923

                      11,500

Provost-guard.................................   205

Total effective detached commands...........   17,794

Total effective, Departments of Northern Virginia, and North Carolina and Southern Virginia.................................   62,875

PETERSBURG, NOVEMBER 10, 1864.

DEPARTMENT OF NORTHERN VIRGINIA.		PRESENT FOR DUTY.	
		Officers.	Enlisted Men.
First Corps, Longstreet.	Pickett's division.................	397	5,986
	Field's division..................	373	4,227
	Hoke's division..................	349	4,956
		1,119	15,169
Third Corps, A. P. Hill.	Heth's division...................	333	4,520
	Wilcox's division.................	375	5,360
	Mahone's division.................	368	4,795
		1,076	14,675
B. R. Johnson's division.........................		529	6,494
Cavalry Corps, Hampton.	Hampton's division...............	96	1,224
	W. H. F. Lee's division............	141	3,123
	Dearing's brigade.................	61	1,303
	Horse artillery...................	3	94
		301	5,744
Artillery corps.................................		249	5,174
First Mil. Dist., Dept. N. C. and So. Va., Brigadier-General H. A. Wise...........................		203	2,271
Provost-guard.................................		21	200
Total..............		3,498	49,727

No return received of troops serving in the Valley of Virginia since October 31, 1864.

PETERSBURG, NOVEMBER 30, 1864.

Total Effective.

First Corps, Longstreet.
- Pickett's division.............. 6,176
- Field's division................ 4,548
- Hoke's division................ 5,273
- Kershaw's division............ 3,414

19,411

Third Corps, A. P. Hill.
- Heth's division................ 4,957
- Wilcox's division............. 5,742
- Mahone's division............ 4,844

15,543

B. R. Johnson's division......................... 6,594

First Military District, Department of North Carolina and Southern Virginia, Brigadier-General Wise... 2,305

Provost-guard.................................. 219

Cavalry Corps, Hampton.
- Hampton's division............ 1,506
- W. H. F. Lee's division........ 3,605
- Dearing's brigade.............. 995
- Horse artillery................ 102

6,208

Artillery corps................................. 6,144

Total effective of all arms, Army Northern Virginia, 56,424

Valley District, Early commanding.
- Early's division............... 2,345
- Rodes's division.............. 2,789
- Gordon's division............. 2,662
- Wharton's division........... 1,859
- Lomax's cavalry.............. 1,846
- Fitz Lee's cavalry............ 1,455

12,956

Total effective in Valley District...............

Total effective in Department of Northern Virginia, 69,380

Of Hampton's cavalry, reported above, 1,298 are dismounted.

PETERSBURG, DECEMBER 20, 1864.

DEPARTMENT OF NORTHERN VIRGINIA.		PRESENT FOR DUTY.	
		Officers.	Enlisted Men.
First Corps, Longstreet.	Pickett's division.................	432	6,365
	Field's division...................	397	4,576
	Hoke's division...................	376	5,517
	Kershaw's division...............	298	3,552
		1,503	20,010
Second Corps, Gordon.	Rodes's division..................	193	3,056
	Early's division...................	133	2,406
	Gordon's division.................	179	2,717
		505	8,179
Third Corps, A. P. Hill.	Mahone's division.................	353	4,544
	Heth's division...................	361	4,905
	Wilcox's division.................	383	5,825
		1,097	15,274

PETERSBURG, DECEMBER 20, 1864—*Continued.*

DEPARTMENT OF NORTHERN VIRGINIA.	PRESENT FOR DUTY.	
	Officers.	Enlisted Men.
B. R. Johnson's division.........................	504	6,692
Cavalry Corps, Hampton. { Hampton's division...............	145	2,431
W. H. F. Lee's division............	158	3,592
Horse artillery...................	3	109
	306	6,132
Artillery corps..................................	266	5,190
First Mil. Dist. Dept. N. C. and So. Va., Brigadier-General H. A. Wise......................	94	520
Provost-guard.................................	22	239
Total..................................	4,297	62,236

PETERSBURG, JANUARY 10, 1865.

DEPARTMENT OF NORTHERN VIRGINIA.	PRESENT FOR DUTY.	
	Officers.	Enlisted Men.
First Corps, Longstreet. { Pickett's division.............	279	4,704
Field's division...............	395	4,569
Kershaw's division............	260	3,140
	934	12,413
Second Corps, Gordon. { Rodes's division..............	203	3,077
Early's division...............	136	2,411
Gordon's division.............	161	2,684
	500	8,172
Third Corps, A. P. Hill. { Mahone's division.............	312	4,536
Heth's division...............	353	4,827
Wilcox's division.............	362	5,827
	1,027	15,190
B. R. Johnson's division........................	433	6,608
Cavalry Corps, Hampton. { Hampton's division...........	133	2,183
W. H. F. Lee's division........	146	3,190
Horse artillery................	3	104
	282	5,477
Artillery corps	256	5,120
Total Army of Northern Virginia..............	3,432	52,980

PETERSBURG; JANUARY 10, 1865—*Continued.*

DEPARTMENT OF NORTHERN VIRGINIA.		PRESENT FOR DUTY.	
		Officers.	Enlisted Men.
Valley District, Early.	Wharton's division............	110	1,914
	Long's artillery........	42	950
	Cavalry......................	Not	reported.
		152	2,864
Brigadier-General J. A. Walker.	Richmond & Danville Railroad defenses......................	110	1,472
Provost-guard...................................		22	219
Total Department of Northern Virginia.........		3,716	57,535

NOTE.—Hoke's division transferred to North Carolina; Conner's brigade, Kershaw's division, transferred to South Carolina. Of cavalry reported, 1,799 are dismounted.

PETERSBURG, JANUARY 31, 1865.

DEPARTMENT OF NORTHERN VIRGINIA.		TOTAL EFFECTIVE.		
First Corps, Longstreet.	Pickett's division......	4,684		
	Field's division........	4,418		
	Kershaw's division.....	3,066		
			12,168	
Second Corps, Gordon.	Rodes's division......	2,914		
	Early's division........	2,319		
	Gordon's division.....	2,529		
			7,762	
Third Corps, A. P. Hill.	Heth's division........	4,319		
	Wilcox's division......	5,840		
	Mahone's division......	4,646		
			14,805	
B. R. Johnson's division...............			6,248	
W. H. F. Lee's division, cavalry.......			4,057	
Artillery corps......................			4,881	
Total effective of all arms, Army of Northern Virginia................				49,921
Valley District, Early.	Wharton's infantry....	1,112		
	Artillery.............	775		
	Cavalry.............	Not	reported.	
			1,887	
J. A. Walker—R. & D. Railroad defenses.			1,438	
Provost-guard.......................			199	
				3,524
Total effective of all arms, Department of Northern Virginia........				53,445

PETERSBURG, FEBRUARY 10, 1865.

DEPARTMENT OF NORTHERN VIRGINIA.	PRESENT FOR DUTY.	
	Officers.	Enlisted Men.
First Corps, Longstreet. Pickett's division	306	4,773
First Corps, Longstreet. Field's division	334	4,453
First Corps, Longstreet. Kershaw's division	227	3,083
	867	12,309
Second Corps, Gordon. Rodes's division	183	2,929
Second Corps, Gordon. Gordon's division	148	2,281
Second Corps, Gordon. Early's division	119	2,151
	450	7,361
Third Corps, A. P. Hill. Mahone's division	284	3,890
Third Corps, A. P. Hill. Heth's division	295	4,190
Third Corps, A. P. Hill. Wilcox's division	316	5,445
	895	13,525
B. R. Johnson's division	426	6,527
W. H. F. Lee's cavalry	137	2,664
Gary's brigade, cavalry	54	1,112
	191	3,776
Total Army of Northern Virginia	2,829	43,498
Valley District, Early. Wharton's infantry	66	1,076
Valley District, Early. Long's artillery	18	390
	84	1,466
J. A. Walker—R. & D. Railroad defenses	100	1,417
Provost-guard and signal corps	27	341
Total Department of Northern Virginia	3,040	46,722

No report of artillery embraced in this return.

PETERSBURG, FEBRUARY 28, 1865.

DEPARTMENT OF NORTHERN VIR- GINIA.		OFFICERS.	ENLISTED MEN.	TOTAL.	
First Corps, Longstreet.	Pickett's division...	304	4,761		
	Field's division.....	341	4,436		
	Kershaw's division..	206	2,967		
		851	12,164		
Second Corps, Gordon.	Gordon's division..	143	2,309		
	Rodes's division....	186	3,022		
	Early's division.....	129	2,292		
		458	7,623		
Third Corps, A. P. Hill.	Mahone's division...	262	3,880		
	Heth's division.....	294	4,324		
	Wilcox's division...	309	5,383		
		865	13,587		
B. R. Johnson's division............		431	6,505		
Effective infantry..............				42,484	
Cavalry Corps.	W. H. F. Lee's division...........	185	3,935		
	Fitz Lee's division...	96	1,825		
Effective cavalry...............				6,041	
Effective artillery..............				5,399	
Total effective of all arms, Army of Northern Virginia............					53,924
Valley District, Early.	Wharton's division, infantry.........	68	1,112		
	Long's division, artillery...........	20	368		
	Lomax's division, cavalry.........	154	1,383		
Total effective.................				3,105	
J. A. Walker.	R. & D. Railroad defenses...........	104	1,414		
Unattached commands..............		42	504		
Total effective, detached commands.				2,064	
					5,169
Total effective of all arms, Department of Northern Virginia.					59,093

By reference to the returns of the Federal armies of the 1st of March, 1865, as given in the report of the Secretary of War to the Thirty-ninth Congress (vol. v., p. 55), I find that General Grant had available at that date, the Army of the Potomac under General Meade, one hundred and three thousand two hundred and seventy-three present for duty; the army in the " Department of Virginia " under General Ord, numbering forty-five thousand nine hundred and eighty-six; and the cavalry force of the Middle Military Division under General Sheridan, twelve thousand nine hundred and eighty strong: making an effective total of all arms of one hundred and sixty-two thousand two hundred and thirty-nine.

There is no return of the Army of Northern Virginia on file in the Archive-Office, at Washington, of later date than that last given. It will be seen that on the 28th of February, 1865, General Lee had available thirty-nine thousand eight hundred and seventy-nine muskets. During the month of March the army lost heavily. In the assault made by General Gordon's troops on the line of the enemy, on the 25th, the Confederate loss was between twenty-five hundred and three thousand. The loss to the army by desertion, in the last thirty days of the siege, was three thousand men; an average of one hundred per day. On the 31st of March, General Lee had therefore but thirty-three thousand muskets, with which to defend a line over thirty miles in length —one thousand men to the mile!

In the engagement at Five Forks on the 1st of April, the divisions of Pickett and Bushrod Johnson were well-nigh annihilated by the Federal turning force, under Sheridan and Warren, which overwhelmed them; the loss sustained there reached seven thousand men.[1] In the encounters at other points on the 31st of March and the 1st of April, and in the general assault on the lines made on the 2d of April, the loss was very heavy, perhaps six thousand men. So that, when General Lee withdrew his army from the

---

[1] The Federals claim to have taken five thousand prisoners.

lines during the night of the 2d of April, he had not over
twenty thousand muskets available. The cavalry had also
suffered heavily, and, of all arms, not over twenty-five thousand men began the retreat that terminated at Appomattox
Court-House.

Speaking in behalf of my former comrades of the Army
of Northern Virginia, I here rest our case, and declare our
readiness to accept the judgment of the world, as to the
genius and skill of the commander, and the valor and endurance of the men, who fought so nobly and fell so bravely,
full of honors, though denied success.

In what I have written, I have endeavored, first, to assist in making clear some matters touching the history of
General Lee, heretofore shrouded in obscurity or doubt;
secondly, to present a statement of the strength of the army
which he commanded, that could be relied upon as accurate.

In regard to the first branch of my undertaking, I need
not that others should remind me of the imperfect manner
of its execution; but, of the matter, and of the spirit in
which I addressed myself to the work, I claim that my only
aim has been historic accuracy. Indeed, I have written as
if under the supervision of General Lee himself, fully realizing that, were that illustrious man now living, he would scorn
any advantage obtained through injustice to others, or the
sacrifice of truth: and this conviction has been present to
my mind as a controlling force through my entire narrative.

In regard to the second branch of my subject, I feel assured that the statement of the strength of the Confederate
army has been presented in such form as to command the
confidence of all. Startling to some as the disparity in numbers between the two armies on certain occasions may appear, it is nevertheless established upon incontrovertible evidence, and makes pardonable the emotions of pride with
which the soldier of the Army of Northern Virginia points
to the achievements of that incomparable body of soldiery,
under its peerless and immortal leader. Had he lived, I have

shown that it was his purpose to prepare for the benefit of posterity, and as a just tribute to the courage and endurance of his men, a true statement of the odds against which they had to contend.   What the designs of an inscrutable but all-wise Providence prevented him from doing, in this particu-lar, I have had the temerity to attempt, and now submit the result of my labor to the judgment of my countrymen, in the hope that in criticising my work they will not lose sight of the purpose by which I have been actuated, or the spirit in which I have performed my task.

ADDRESS

ON THE CHARACTER OF GENERAL R. E. LEE,

Delivered in Richmond, on Wednesday, January 19, 1876, the Anniversary of
General Lee's Birth, by Captain John Hampden Chamberlayne.

FELLOW-CITIZENS : I shall not obtrude upon you apologies
or explanations, as if I had the orator's established fame to
lose, or looked that future fame to win. You are not come
to hear of my small hopes or fears. Yet, to you, and to the
gravity of the occasion, it is due to say that I appear before you
on sudden order, to my sense of duty hardly less imperative
than those famous commands under which we have so often
marched at " early dawn."

By telegraph, on last Saturday night, this duty was laid upon me, and I come with little of preparation, and less of ability,
to attempt a theme that might task the powers of Bossuet or
exhaust an Everett's rhetoric.

It can scarcely be needful to rehearse before you the facts
of our commander's life. They have become, from least to
greatest, parts of history, and an ever-growing number of books
record that he was born in 1807, at Stratford, in Westmoreland
County, of a family ancient and honorable in the mother-country,
in the Old Dominion, and in the State of Virginia ; that he was
appointed a cadet at the United States Military Academy in
1825, and was graduated first in his class, and commissioned
lieutenant of engineers ; that he served upon the staff of General Scott through the brilliant campaign from Vera Cruz to

the city of Mexico, was thrice brevetted for gallant and meritorious conduct, and was declared by General Scott to have borne a chief part in the counsels and the battles which ended with the triumph of our arms ; that he was promoted lieutenant-colonel of cavalry, and served for years upon the Southwestern frontier; that he was in 1861 called to Washington as one of a board to revise the army regulations ; and that on the 20th day of April, 1861, four days after the withdrawal of Virginia from the Union, he resigned his commission in the United States Army, and that he became commander-in-chief of Virginia's forces, and thereafter accepted the commission of general in the army of the Confederate States.

Still more familiar to you than these facts are the events of which you and I had personal knowledge : how Lee organized, patiently and skillfully, the raw resources of Virginia ; how he directed the coast defenses of the South Atlantic States, and how he labored against a thousand difficulties in the mountains of West Virginia, serenely accepting without a murmur the popular verdict on what ignorant presumption adjudged a failure.   In June of 1862 he was at length placed in a command to meet whose vast responsibility his life had been the preparation, and at once his name became forever linked with that Army of Northern Virginia which met and mastered army after army, baffled McClellan, and destroyed successively Pope, Burnside, and Hooker ; which twice invaded the enemy's country, and which, when at last against it were thrown all the resources of the United States, Grant in its front and Sherman in its rear, Europe for their recruiting-ground, and a boundless credit for their military chest, still stood for eleven months defiantly at bay, concentrated on itself the whole resources of the United States, and surrendered at Appomattox eight thousand starving men to the combined force of two great armies whose chiefs had long despaired to conquer it by skill or daring, and had worn it away by weight of numbers and brutal exchange of many lives for one.   We all know, too, how the famous soldier sheathed his sword, and without a word of repining, without a look to show the grief that was breaking his heart and sapping the springs of his noble life, accepted the duty that came to him, and bent to his new task, as guide and teacher of boys, the powers which had wielded the strength of armies and almost redressed the balances of unequal fate.

Such are the leading facts, in barest outline, of the great life that began sixty-nine years ago to-day. Well known as they are, it is wise to recall them when we gather as we have gathered here. In these hurrying days men pass swiftly away from human sight, the multitude of smaller figures vanishing behind the curtain of forgetfulness, the few mighty ones soon wrapped in the hazy atmosphere of the heroic heights, enlarged, it may be, but ofttimes dim and distorted, always afar off, unfamiliar, not human, but superhuman, demi-gods rather than men; our wonder and our despair, who should be our reverence and our inspiration.

Thus has it already been with him who lies at Mount Vernon. Let it be our care, men of this generation, that it be not so in our day with him who lies at Lexington ; let it be our care to show him often to those who rise around us to take our place, to show him not only in his great deeds and his famous victories, but also as citizen and as man.

The task is hard to divide what is essentially one, and Lee so bore himself in his great office as that the man was never lost in the soldier. Never of him could it be said that he was like the dyer's hand, subdued to what he worked in : always the sweet human quality tempered his stoic virtue, always beneath the soldier's breast beat the tender, loving heart.

Most of us here have seen and known him, if not in his splendid youth, fit at once to charm the eye of the Athenian multitude and to awe a Roman Senate, yet in his maturer years, when time and care had worn his body but to show more glorious the lofty soul within. Among us and ours his life was led, so blameless as might become a saint, so tender as might become a woman, so simple as might become the little children " of whom is the kingdom of heaven." So consistent was that life, so devoted to duty, without a glance to right or left, so fixed on the golden rule, adopted once and forever, that his biographer, even now in a time of passion and distorted truth, hesitates what to choose for his highest praise—lingering in turn over Lee the son, Lee the husband, Lee the father, Lee the friend. Idle, then, it were for me to picture him in all the relations he bore to those around him, and worse than idle were I to follow what is much the fashion nowadays and make a study of Lee the Christian, pry with curious glance into the sacred chamber wherein man kneels to his God, or dare to touch the awful veil which fools are swift to rend.

" But," says the critic, " private virtue is not for public use; a Torquemada may be gentle in his home, and a Stuart seek to enslave his people, yet lead a life of chastity."

'Tis true, but still our great commander shines flawless and perfect, at once in the quiet beams of the household hearth and in the fierce light that beats upon the throne of him born to be king of men.

Let one great example show it. None but those who know the power of lofty ambition can tell what vast temptation beset our leader ; none can know the heroism of the decision in the dark days of 1861. He was the favorite soldier of all who followed Scott ; he was the picked and chosen man for high command in the armies of the United States. He was besought almost with tears by him he reverenced as a second father ; to him was tendered the *bâton* of general-in-chief. Who can tell what visions trooped upon his sight—of power, that dearest boon to the powerful, of fame world-wide, of triumph, not easy but certain ? And who can tell but fairer dreams than these assailed him ; hope, nay, almost belief, that he and he alone might play the noble part of *pacificator* and *redintegrator patriæ*, that he might heal the wounds of civil strife, and be hailed by North and South as worthy the oaken garland ?

He had been more or less than human had not these thoughts, or such as these, arisen when he strove through days and bitter nights to find his duty.

He, we must remember, was wedded to no theory ; his mind grasped concrete truth rather than abstractions. His horizon was bounded by no lines of neighborhood or of States. He knew the men of the North, as well as of the South ; he had maturely weighed the wealth of the one and the poverty of the other. Few knew so well as he, none better, the devotion we could offer to any cause, but he knew likewise the stubborn, deep-resting strength of the Northern will that we took for a passing whim. He had all his life obeyed and respected the organized, concentrated form of the Union; and he, the pupil of Scott, the follower of Washington, the son of Light-Horse Harry, might and should and did pause long. Paused long, to decide forever—to decide with never a look backward, with never a regret, even when the end had come, darker than his fears had pictured.

Cast away all, to obey the voice of Virginia, his country; to defend Virginia, his mother. Scarcely twice since the world began has mortal man been called to make such choice.

Will not history consent, will not mankind applaud, when we still uphold our principles as right, our cause as just, our country to be honored, when those principles had for disciple, that cause for defender, that country for son, Robert Lee?

The day has by no means come to fix with absolute precision the rank of Lee among the world's great soldiers. But the day will come, and it is ours to gather and preserve and certify the facts to be the record before the dread tribunal of time.

Turning, then, to the soldiership of Lee : from first to last, we see his labor and exactness, giving always the power to gain from every means its utmost result. Thus he so pursued the sciences which underlie the soldier's art that he entered the army fully equipped with all that theory could teach, and while yet a subaltern was more than once intrusted with tasks of the engineers' bureau which had baffled the skill of men far older and more experienced. The same qualities were shown when he first saw actual war. To us, who look back across the field of a gigantic strife, of a struggle where not brigades nor divisions but great armies were the units, where States were fortified camps and a continent the battle-ground—to us that march on Mexico seems as small as it is, in fact, far off in time and space. But small and great are relative, and the little army of Scott which gathered on the sands of Vera Cruz was little in much the same sense as that other army, of Cortez, whose footsteps it followed and whose prowess it rivaled. In that campaign Lee's soldiership first found fit field. It was he whose skill gave us the quick foothold of Vera Cruz.   At Cerro Gordo and Contreras his was no mean part of the plan and its accomplishment.   At the city of Mexico it was his soldier's eye and soldier's heart which saw and dared what Cortez had seen and dared before, to turn the enemy's strongest position, and assault as well by the San Cosme as by the Belen gateway, a movement greatly hazardous, but, once executed, decisive.   In the endless roll of wars that campaign of Mexico must always remain to the judicious critic masterly in conception and superb in execution. But to us it is memorable chiefly as the training-school whose pupils were to ply their art on a wider scale to ends more terrible, and Winfield Scott selected from them all Robert E. Lee as the chosen soldier.

The time was soon to come when he should try conclusions with many of that brilliant band, and prove himself the master of each in turn—of McClellan, of Burnside, of Hooker, of Pope, of Meade, of Grant, of whomsoever could be found to lead them by the millions he confronted.   When the War of Secession began, you all remember how for a time Lee held subordinate place, and how, when what seemed chance gave him command of the forces defending Richmond from the hundred thousand men who could hear, if they would, the bells of our churches and almost the hum of our streets—you all remember how the home-staying critic found fault with him, how he was described as a closet-soldier and a handler of spade and mattock, rather than of gun and bayonet.   Sudden and swift was the surprise when the great plan disclosed itself, and the guns at the Meadow Bridges of the Chickahominy cleared the way for the first of those mighty blows which sent McClellan in hopeless rout to the shelter of his shipping, thence to hurry as he might to the rescue of Pope's bewildered divisions, and to organize home-guards in the defenses of Washington.   That single campaign of the Seven Days is itself fame.   To amuse an army outnumbering his own by fifty thousand ; to watch with a large detachment lest that army should make a junction with the divisions at Fredericksburg ; to bring Jackson's skill and Jackson's devoted men to his aid ; to cross a marshy and often impracticable stream ; to attack McClellan on his flank and to roll up his army like a scroll, while, at each step gained, his enemy should be weaker and himself be stronger and in stronger position, yet at the same time to guard lest his enemy should break his centre as Napoleon pierced the Russians on Austerlitz field —such was the problem. You know, all the world knows, its execution. Despite the errors of subordinates ; despite the skill of his opponent, a soldier truly great in defense ; despite the rawness of many of his troops ; despite the lack in the general officers of the skill necessary to movements so delicate ; and despite the inferiority of his force, Lee succeeded fully in his main object, relieved Richmond, inflicted on his enemy losses materially immense and morally infinite ; in seven days absolutely undid what McClellan took six months to do, and by a single combination threw back his enemy from the hills in sight of Richmond to a defensive line in Washington's suburbs. This campaign, for its audacity, its wide combination, its insight into the opponent's character, its self-reliance, its vigor of execution, and its astonishing results, may be safely compared with the best campaigns of the greatest masters in the art of war—with Frederick's Leuthen, to which it bears as much likeness as a campaign of days can bear to a battle of hours, or with that greater feat, the amazing concentration by Washington of contingents from New York and from North Carolina, of new levies from the Virginia Valley, and of a French fleet from the West Indies, to besiege and to capture the army of Cornwallis.

It is argued that Lee was strong only in defense, and was averse to taking the offensive. Nothing could be more false. He was to prove in the last year of the war his fertility of defensive resource and his unrivaled tenacity of resistance. But his genius was aggressive. Witness the bold transfer of his army from Richmond to the Rapidan, while McClellan's troops still rested on the James River. Witness the audacity of detaching Jackson from the Rappahannock line to seize Manassas Junction and the road to Washington in Pope's rear. Witness the magnificent swoop on Harper's Ferry, of which accident gave to McClellan the knowledge and by which timidity forbade him to profit. Witness that crowning glory of his audacity, the change of front to attack Hooker, and that march around what Hooker called "the best position in America, held by the finest army on the planet." Witness his invasion of Pennsylvania, a campaign whose only fault was the generous fault of over-confidence in an army whose great deeds might, if anything, excuse it—an over-confidence, as we ourselves know, felt by every man he led, and which made us reckless of all difficulties, ready to think that to us nothing was impossible. He was a commander who had met no equal; we were an army who saw in half the guns of our train the spoil of the enemy, who bore upon our flags the blazon of consistent victory. If he and we confided in our daring, and trusted to downright fighting for what strategy might have safely won, who shall blame us and which shall blame the other? It was a fault, if fault there were, such as in a soldier leans to virtue's side; it was the fault of Marlborough at Malplaquet, of the Great Frederick at Torgau, of Napoleon at Borodino. It is the famous fault of the column of Fontenoy, and the generous haste that led Hampden to his death.

Lee chose no defensive of his own will. None knew better than he that axiom of the military art which finds the logical end of defense in surrender. None knew better than he that Fabius had never earned his fame by the policy some attribute to him, nor saved his country by retreats, however regular, or the skill, however great, to choose positions only to abandon them. The defensive was not his chosen field, but he was fated to conduct a defensive campaign rivaled by few and surpassed by none in history. Of that wonderful work the details are yet to be gathered, but the outlines are known the world over. The tremendous onset of Lee in the tangled Wilderness upon an enemy three times his force, who fancied him retreating; the grim wrestle of Spottsylvania; the terrible repulse of Cold Harbor, from which the veteran commanders of Grant shrank back aghast — these great actions will be known so long as war shall be studied, and future generations will read with admiration of that battle-field of seventy miles, where Lee with fifty-one thousand men confronted Grant with his one hundred and ninety thousand—attacked him wherever he showed uncovered front, killed, wounded, and captured, more men than his own army numbered; and, in a campaign of thirty-five days, forced the most tenacious soldier of the Union armies to abandon utterly his line of attack, to take a new position always open to him but never chosen, and to exchange the warfare of the open field for the slow and safe approach of the earthwork and the siege.

They will read, too, that in the midst of this campaign Lee was bold to spare from his little army force enough to take once more the offensive, to traverse once more the familiar Valley, to break once more through the gate of the Potomac, and to insult with the fires of his bivouacs the capital city of his enemy. Reading these things, they will refuse to believe, what we know, that men were found here and now to call this marvelous campaign a retreat.

The truth is, that Lee took a real defensive, if at all, only in the trenches of Petersburg ; was driven to that defensive not by one army nor by many armies in succession, but by the combined force of the armies in his front and in his rear.   Vicksburg it was, not Cemetery Hill, which baffled the Army of Northern Virginia ; at Nashville and Atlanta, not from the lines of Petersburg, came the deadly blows ; and the ragged remnant of Appomattox surrendered not to the valor or skill of the men they had so often met and overcome, but to the men they had never seen, and yielded neither to stubborn Grant nor braggart Sheridan, but to the triumphant hosts of Rosecrans, of Thomas, and of Sherman.

It is not hard, then, my friends, to see that history will hold Lee to be a great soldier, wise in counsel, patient in preparation, swift in decision, terrible in onset, tenacious of hold, sullen in retreat, a true son of that Berserker race that rushed from the bosom of Europe's darkest age, furious to fight, lovers of battle, destined to sweep away the old world and to mould the modern.

Rightly to estimate his power as commander is not and may never be possible.   There is no second term of comparison.   He was in a position as novel as were the conditions of a war where the railroad existed, but the highway was not ; where telegraphs conveyed orders, yet primeval forests still stood to conceal armies ; where concentration was possible at a speed unknown to war before, but where concentration might easily starve itself before it could strike its enemy.

Strange as the material, were the moral conditions of Lee's command. He was hampered by political considerations ; he was trammeled by the supreme importance of one city ; and, above all, on him was complete responsibility, but never commensurate power. To the integrity of his army, to the *morale* of half his force, the successful defense of the South and Southwest was essential, and on operations in which he had no voice turned the issue of his campaigns.

Of these things account will yet be taken, let us be sure of that ; for though in barbarous ages conquered peoples write no histories, yet, as the world grows older, history grows more and more a judge, less and less a witness and advocate ; more and more to every cause that appeal lies open which Francis Bacon, of Verulam, made " to future ages and other countries."

Fit is it that we trust to that great verdict, seeing that nothing less than the tribunal of mankind can judge this man, who was born not for a period, but for all time ; not for a country, but for the world ; not for a people, but for the human race.

Not for him shall the arch of triumph rise ; not for him columns of victory, telling through monumental bronze the hideous tale of tears and blood that grins from the skull-pyramids of Dahomey. Not to his honor shall extorted tributes carve the shaft or mould the statue ; but this day a grateful people give of their poverty gladly, that in pure marble, or time-defying bronze, future generations may see the counterfeit presentment of this man—the ideal and bright consummate flower of our civilization ; not an Alexander, it may be ; nor Napoleon, nor Timour, nor Churchill—greater far than they, thank Heaven— the brother and the equal of Sidney and of Falkland, of Hampden and of Washington !

THE END.

NOTES.

Page 11. Taylor wrote later that he was having breakfast in Richmond's Spottswood Hotel when he first saw Lee. "He was then at the zenith of his physical beauty," Taylor remembered. "Admirably proportioned, of graceful and dignified carriage, with strikingly handsome features, bright and penetrating eyes, his iron-gray hair closely cut, his face cleanly shaven except a mustache, he appeared every inch a soldier and a man born to command." W. H. Taylor, *General Lee: His Campaigns in Virginia, 1861–1865; With Personal Reminiscences* (Norfolk, 1906), pp. 21–22. Hereafter cited as Taylor, *General Lee.*

Page 16. John A. Washington was a grand-nephew of George Washington and the last member of that distinguished family to reside at Mount Vernon. This Virginia aristocrat was a long-time friend of Lee's. Shortly after their arrival in western Virginia, Lee, Washington, and Taylor went reconnoitering a half-mile in advance of the Confederate lines. Suddenly three Southern soldiers broke from the thickets and angrily leveled muskets at the mounted trio. Then, with obvious embarrassment, they explained to Lee that they had seen three officers scouting near the Confederate positions. Thinking them to be Federals, the Rebel soldiers had set out to capture them. A. L. Long, *Memoirs of Robert E. Lee* (New York, 1886), p. 121. Hereafter cited as Long, *Memoirs.*

Page 17. Taylor's pessimistic report of the army's condition was no exaggeration. A North Carolina regiment lost one-third of its strength from disease before it ever encountered a Federal soldier. In a letter home, Lee himself observed: "Our poor sick, I know, suffer much. They bring it on themselves by not doing what they are told. They are worse than children, for the latter can be forced." Douglas S. Freeman, *Lee's Lieutenants* (New York, 1942–44), I, 556.

Page 32. His jealousy notwithstanding, Henry Wise was an audacious and forceful commander. Once during this campaign the Federals were advancing in force against Wise's thin line when the wiry general rode up to a young artillery lieutenant and ordered the officer to open fire on the Yankees. The young officer protested; the forest in his front was so dense, he stated, that he could "do no execution" to the Federals. "Damn the execution, sir," Wise barked, "it's the *noise* that we want!" Taylor, *General Lee,* pp. 33–34.

Page 34. Apparently the weather at this time turned bitterly cold. Lee, who rarely displayed any reaction to extreme temperatures, nevertheless asked Taylor one night to pool blankets and sleep together in an effort to keep warm. *Ibid.,* pp. 31–32.

Page 35. Quite in contrast to Taylor's analysis, E. A. Pollard, the fiery editor of the Richmond *Examiner,* displayed his contempt of Lee's management of affairs in western Virginia by writing: "The most remarkable circumstance of this campaign was, that it was conducted by a general who had never fought a battle, who had a pious horror of guerillas, and whose extreme tenderness of blood induced him to depend exclusively upon the resources of strategy to essay the achievement of victory without the cost of life." E. A. Pollard, *The First Year of the War* (Richmond, 1862), p. 191. Throughout the war Lee was extremely self-denying in the matter of food. He could not bring himself to enjoy a full-course meal when his army was in a half-starved condition. His usual lunch, for example, consisted of cabbage boiled in salt water. Douglas S. Freeman, *R. E. Lee* (New York, 1934–35), III, 251. Hereafter cited as Freeman, *Lee.*

Page 37. After assuming command of the Department of South Carolina, Georgia, and East Florida, with headquarters at Coosawhatchie, S. C., Lee named as his staff: Capt. T. A. Washington, Adjutant-General; Capt. Walter H. Taylor, Assistant Adjutant-General; Capt. Joseph C. Ives, Chief Engineer; Lt. Col. William G. Gill, Ordnance Officer; and Joseph Manigault, Aide-de-camp. U. S. War Dept. (comp.), *War of the Rebellion: A Compilation of the Official Records of the Union and Confederate Armies* (Washington, 1880–1901), Ser. I, Vol. VI, 312. Hereafter cited as *OR;* all references will be to Ser. I. The fire to which Taylor referred broke out on the evening of December 11 and swept through the city of Charleston. Lee and Taylor both were compelled to leave their dinner and flee to safety when the flames enveloped the Mills House. See Taylor, *General Lee,* pp. 40–41; Long, *Memoirs,* pp. 135–36.

Page 40. Many writers assert that Seven Pines and Fair Oaks were two battles, and that the latter was a comparatively mild engagement which occurred on June 1. Taylor's critical remarks about Jeb Stuart were seconded by E. Porter Alexander in his *Military Memoirs of a Confederate* (New York, 1907; Bloomington, Ind., 1962), pp. 168–70. Yet cavalrymen were quick to defend Stuart's conduct near Harrison's Landing. See H. B. McClellan, *The Life and Campaigns of Maj.-Gen. J. E. B. Stuart* (Richmond, 1885; and as *I Rode with Jeb Stuart*, Bloomington, Ind., 1958), pp. 84–85.

Page 43. In his second narrative Taylor bluntly stated of Stuart's action: "The firing of the little howitzer was a mistake. Every effort should have been made to hasten the march of the infantry and the field-artillery; and in the meantime only a squadron or two of cavalry for the purpose of observation should have occupied Evelington Heights. . . . Only a few hours more and the infantry, with field-batteries, would have been up, and would have made sure of the plateau commanding the position held by the enemy." As substantiation, Taylor referred to Silas Casey's testimony, p. 42n. *General Lee,* p. 83.

Page 44. For a pointed discussion on whether McClellan's move after Gaines' Mill was a "change of base" or a panicky retreat, see Kenneth P. Williams, *Lincoln Finds A General* (New York, 1949–59), I, 230–33.

Page 52. Elderly but gallant Isaac G. Seymour was colonel of the 6th Louisiana. He was temporarily in command of a Louisiana brigade at Gaines' Mill, and was killed early in the fighting. Richard Taylor succeeded him and went on to become one of the Confederacy's outstanding generals.

Page 57. Taylor, Long, Fitzhugh Lee and others who penned studies of Lee prior to the publication of the. *Official Records* believed and stated that Lee laid plans to threaten Washington and invade the North early in July, 1862. Taylor repeated this assumption in *General Lee,* pp. 85–86. In reality, Freeman concluded, Lee's planning "was not a matter of prescience or even of precision. Knowing comparatively little of the intentions of his opponents, he had to shape his plan, step by step, as his information accumulated." *Lee,* II, 259.

Page 58. After Second Manassas Taylor wrote home that "the Yankees fought as if in earnest." Quoted in Freeman, *Lee,* II, 346. In his *General Lee,* pp. 115–16, Taylor related in detail the September 1 accident to Lee, whereby the commander was thrown from his horse, sprained both wrists, and broke several small bones in one hand. For several days thereafter, Lee, with each arm in a sling, was compelled to ride in an ambulance. "This was a sore trial to the general's patience," Taylor observed.

Page 67. The question of responsibility for the now-famous "Lost Order" has occasioned over the past ninety years an unwarranted flood of charges and countercharges. While Gen. Harvey Hill has been the usual target for censure, extant evidence seems to exonerate him from blame. Hill received his copy of Special Order No. 191 from Lee and kept it until his death. It is now preserved in the North Carolina Department of Archives and History. Jackson, under the impression that Hill was temporarily in his command, wrote a copy of the orders and sent them by courier to his colleague and brother-in-law. Hill never received this copy, which was undoubtedly the one discovered by the Federals. For an example of drastically conflicting opinions on this issue, see Edward A. Pollard, *The Lost Cause* (New York, 1867), p. 314; *The Land We Love,* IV (1868), 270–84.

Page 68. For soldiers' statements verifying Taylor's description of straggling prior to Sharpsburg, see Luther W. Hopkins, *From Bull Run to Appomattox* (Baltimore, 1908), p. 51; *Southern Historical Society Papers,* XII (1884), 507. Hereafter cited as *SHSP.* See also Taylor, *General Lee,* pp. 130–31.

Page 70. In a letter to his sister on September 21, 1862, Taylor stated in part: "The fight of the 17th has taught us the value of our men, who can, even when weary with constant marching and fighting, and when on short rations, contend with and resist three times their own numbers. . . . Congress must provide for reinforcing us, and then we will be enabled to realize their sanguine expectation." Walter H. Taylor letters, in possession of Miss Janet F. Taylor, Norfolk, Virginia. Hereafter cited as Taylor MSS. Years later Taylor wrote of Sharpsburg: "At times it appeared as if disaster were inevitable, but succor never failed, and night found General Lee's lines unbroken and his army still defiant." *General Lee,* p. 134.

Page 73. Taylor originally placed Lee's strength at Sharpsburg at 35,255 men. He later revised the figure to 36,175 troops. *SHSP,* XXIV (1896), 272. Lee, in his own report, calculated his army at "less than 40,000 men." *OR,* XIX, pt. 1, 151.

Page 74. In spite of A. P. Hill's jubilant report of the September 20 rearguard action, Federal casualties numbered only 269 men. Many of these were shot as they splashed frantically back across the Potomac in an effort to escape Hill's heavy onslaught. *OR,* XIX, pt. 1, 204, 340, 350, 982.

Page 76. Lee's second daughter, Annie, died on October 20, 1862, at the age of twenty-three. She had gone to Warren White Sulphur Spring, N. C., for a short vacation and succumbed there after a very brief illness.

Page 77. Maj. Giles Cook gave a more dramatic account of the tiff between Lee and Taylor in *Confederate Veteran,* XXIV (1916), 234. In this version Lee stopped his adjutant at the tent opening and stated: "Colonel Taylor, if I, with all the care of the army on my shoulders, should forget myself, I hope you will not forget yourself." According to Giles, "the Colonel was melted, and the papers were duly signed." See also Freeman, *Lee,* III, 228.

Page 82. Shortly after the Fredericksburg slaughter, a Confederate soldier walking across the battlefield stopped to remove the boots from a Federal officer who lay prone and still on the ground. The Southern soldier was tugging earnestly on one boot when the Federal suddenly raised his head and cursed. Quickly regaining his composure, the Confederate replied, "Beg pardon, sir, I thought you had gone above," and then nonchalantly walked away. Taylor, *General Lee,* p. 149. In the wintry days immediately after the battle of Fredericksburg, Lee refused all offers tendered him to take quarters in several nearby homes. He did not wish, one Confederate officer explained, "to fare any better than his men did. There was no pomp or circumstance about his headquarters, and no sign of the rank of the occupant, other than the Confederate flag displayed in front of the tent of Colonel Taylor, the Adjutant-General." Francis W. Dawson, *Reminiscences of Confederate Service, 1861–1865* (Charleston, S. C., 1882), pp. 87–88.

Page 85. Capt. Murray F. Taylor of A. P. Hill's staff rode to Lee's headquarters with the news of the wounding of Jackson and Hill. As Lee at the time was resting, the staff officer gave the ominous report to Walter Taylor, who was standing before a camp fire. Taylor at once hastened to Lee's tent, and the General rushed out to get the news firsthand. *Confederate Veteran,* XII (1904), 493.

Page 92. That Taylor considered Stuart's absence from the field at Gettysburg as a major reason for the Confederate defeat is more apparent in his *General Lee,* pp. 183–86, 210–11. On the other hand, outspoken John Mosby, in *The Memoirs of Colonel John S. Mosby* (Bloomington, Ind., 1959), pp. 218–20, 236–38, went to great lengths to refute Taylor's remarks. Taylor was nevertheless optimistic as Lee's army swung through Pennsylvania. Writing home on June 29, he asserted: "With God's help we expect to take a step or two toward an honorable peace." Taylor MSS.

Page 95. Taylor used essentially the same words in relating this incident in *SHSP,* IV (1877), 83, 127, and in *General Lee,* p. 190.

Page 100. Longstreet's postwar letter to Taylor referred to charges levied by Bishop-General William Nelson Pendleton, who led the anti-Longstreet forces in the vituperative and postwar literary battle of Gettysburg. See James Longstreet, *From Manassas to Appomattox,* edited by James I. Robertson, Jr. (Bloomington, Ind., 1960), pp. xxi–xxii, xxvi, 377–80; Taylor, *General Lee,* pp. 194–203.

Page 103. For Longstreet's opposition to Lee's plan, as outlined by Taylor, see *From Manassas to Appomattox,* p. 386.

Pages 111–12. As the strength of the opposing armies at Gettysburg has always been a point of much discussion and controversy, it is not surprising that Taylor on three occasions gave contradictory figures. In this book he put Lee's battle strength at 68,352 men, as opposed to Meade's 112,000 Federals. Earlier, in *SHSP,* IV (1877), 246, he gave Lee 67,000 men at the height of the campaign in contrast to 105,000 Federals. In *General Lee,* p. 210, he estimated Lee's "maximum strength" at 74,451 troops, and the Federal army at 104,256 men. For this last set of figures, he relied on the *Official Records* rather than on his own notes.

Page 115. Taylor and Lee both exhibited a surprisingly high morale in the weeks following the Gettysburg Campaign. Taylor was convinced that the army fought better on Southern soil. As he stated in a letter of July 17, the Confederates "are not accustomed to operating in a country where the people are inimical to them." On August 8 he wrote home exuberantly: "This is a grand old army! . . . No despondency here, though we hear of it in Richmond." Taylor MSS. And although rations at this time were far from plentiful, Lee would often finish a meal by leaning back in his chair and remarking jovially to his messmate: "Well, Colonel Taylor, we are just as well off as if we had feasted on the best in the land; our hunger is appeased, and I am satisfied." Taylor, *General Lee*, p. 222.

Page 116. John A. Sloan echoed Taylor's sentiments of the Bristoe Station fight by asserting that "a worse managed affair . . . did not take place during the war." *Reminiscences of the Guilford Grays* (Washington, N. C., 1883), p. 74. On the morning after the battle, a saddened Lee rode over the field with Powell Hill and listened patiently as his lieutenant apologetically recounted the particulars. With measured words having all the overtones of a rebuke, Lee cut off the conversation by stating: "Well, well, General, bury these poor men and let us say no more about it." Long, *Memoirs*, p. 311. Taylor himself bemoaned in a letter of November 15 to his sister: "I only wish the general [Lee] had good lieutenants; we miss Jackson and Longstreet terribly." Taylor MSS.

Page 120. Taylor's letter of November 26 is misdated and should read November 25. In that same letter he expressed the fervent hope: "With God's help there shall be a Second Chancellorsville as there was a Second Manassas." The subsequent Mine Run Campaign did not prove so fruitful for the Confederates.

Page 122. In his book Taylor omitted one striking incident relative to Lee's character. Lee left his army in December, 1863, and journeyed to Richmond for consultations with President Davis and other Confederate officials. He received a hero's welcome on his arrival in the Southern capital, and was constantly treated as the Confederacy's most distinguished hero. Back at field headquarters, several staff officers began to speculate whether Lee would stay in Richmond and enjoy the first Christmas with his family since 1859 or whether he would return to the field. Confiding his own opinion to his fiancée, Taylor wrote on December 20: "It will be more in accordance with his peculiar character if he leaves for the army just before the great anniversary; he is so very apt to suppress or deny his personal desire when it conflicts with the performance of his duty." Taylor MSS. On the following day, Lee rode into camp to rejoin his troops.

Page 123. While Gen. Meade willingly forwarded to Lee a statement by Kilpatrick repudiating the document discovered on Dahlgren's body, Meade confided privately to his wife: "I regret to say Kilpatrick's reputation, and collateral evidence in my possession, rather go against this theory. However, I was determined my skirts should be clear, so I promptly disavowed having ever authorized, sanctioned or approved of any act not required by military necessity, and in accordance with the usages of war." *The Life and Letters of George Gordon Meade* (New York, 1913), II, 190–91.

Page 125. Writing home on April 24, 1864, Taylor expressed the conviction that the army was never "in better trim than now. There is no overweening confidence, but a calm, firm and positive determination to be victorious, with God's help." A week later he added that the forthcoming campaign would be the decisive one of the war. "The beginning of the end is, I believe, at hand. . . . Never did matters look so bright for us." Taylor MSS.

Page 126. Lee's health showed a marked improvement as the time neared for the 1864 spring campaign. "Colonel," he remarked to Taylor, "we have got to whip them; we must whip them, and it has already made me better to think of it." Taylor observed that Lee seemed very anxious to do battle with "the present idol of the North." Taylor to Bettie Saunders, April 3, 1864, *ibid.*

Pages 127–28. In the now-famous incident of Confederate soldiers beseeching Lee to go to the rear out of danger, Taylor did his share of persuasion by taking from Lee's hand the regimental flag which the General had intended to use in leading the charge. "Memoirs of Henry Heth," Alderman Library, University of Virginia. See also Taylor, *General Lee,* pp. 233–34.

Page 130. Taylor omitted in his narrative mention of his own conduct during the May 10 struggle near Spotsylvania. Shortly after 6 P.M., Federal infantry smashed through Doles's brigade and threatened to turn Lee's whole line. Lee prepared to ride to the sector, but his staff insisted that it was too dangerous. Obviously dejected, the General muttered: "Then you must see to it that the ground is recovered." In a flash Taylor was on his horse and riding into the midst of the fighting. He dismounted, seized a flag, and led a group of Confederates in a counterattack that succeeded in stunting the Federal advance until nightfall, when the bluecoats withdrew back to their works. Freeman, *Lee,* III, 313–14.

Page 131. The catastrophe at Spotsylvania jolted the morale of Lee's army; yet, Taylor wrote home on May 15, "we are determined to make our next success all the greater to make amends for this disaster. Our men are in good heart and condition, our confidence, certainly mine, unimpaired. Grant is beating his head against a wall." Taylor MSS.

Page 135. Of Cold Harbor Taylor subsequently stated: "The loss of the enemy was frightful to contemplate; the ground in our front was covered with their dead and wounded. The Confederate guns controlled the situation, and it took General Grant two days to make up his mind to ask a truce that he might bury his dead and care for his wounded." *General Lee,* p. 248. In a more flippant style, Taylor told his sweetheart on June 9, 1864: "Old U. S. Grant is pretty tired of it—at least it appears so. We are in excellent trim—men in fine spirits and ready for a renewal of the fight whenever the signal is given." Taylor MSS.

Page 136. Throughout his correspondence, it is apparent that Taylor had little regard or respect for Jubal A. Early. He was certain that a man as void of religious feelings as Early would have little success in the field. On July 10, after Early's scheme to take Washington seemed destined to failure, Taylor cried out in a letter home: "Oh! If Jackson were only where he is." Taylor MSS.

Page 138. The Confederates knew well in advance that the Federals were digging at least one tunnel under the Southern lines. The seriousness of the move notwithstanding, many of the Rebels made fun of the expedition. For example, Taylor wrote in a letter of July 25 that a new conscript was told to go on the main street of Petersburg and listen carefully. When he heard the roar of an approaching locomotive, he should look down at the street, where he soon would be able to see train smoke seep up through the cracks in the cobblestones. *Ibid.* On August 1, however, a truce was called to bury the dead around the Crater. Many Confederate officers, Taylor included, took this opportunity to view the great chasm made by the explosion. "Gruesome indeed" was Taylor's initial impression. "The force of the explosion had carried earth, guns, accouterments, and men some distance skyward, the whole coming down in an inextricable mass; portions of the bodies of the poor victims were to be seen protruding from immense blocks of earth. . . . The bottom of the pit or crater was covered with dead, white and black intermingled, a horrible sight." *General Lee,* p. 258.

Page 140. On October 6 Taylor informed his fiancée: "Though our men have not altogether the old spirit, there still are many who will do anything to be expected of mortals; and if this fraction is properly supported, all is well." Taylor MSS. Cf. Taylor, *General Lee,* pp. 264–67.

Page 142. Brig. Gen. Archibald Gracie, Jr., a native of Alabama, and two other Confederate officers were killed on December 3 when a shell from Battery Morton exploded in their midst. In one of those freak incidents of history, Gracie had in his pocket furlough papers to visit his wife and child in Richmond—but had missed the train he was scheduled to take.

Page 145. The attack on the Federal·line by Gordon's command referred to the March 25 Confederate assault on Fort Stedman. This last offensive by the Army of Northern Virginia failed and cost "Lee's Miserables" close to 5,000 casualties. See Freeman, *Lee's Lieutenants,* III, 645–53. Although desertion in Lee's army at this time was unbelievably high (779 soldiers crept away in one ten-day period early in March), Taylor's patriotism remained unbounded. When a South Carolina regiment on March 31 moved out at double-quick to stop a Federal probe, Taylor's emotions got the best of him. He left Lee, rode out in front of the tattered gray line and, waving his hat over his head, shouted to the Confederates: "Come ahead, men! God bless you! I love every one of you!" *OR,* XLVI, pt. 2, 1292–93; *Confederate Veteran,* VII (1899), 464.

Page 149. On April 2, at the comfortable home of William Turnbull near Petersourg, Lee dictated to Taylor the fateful announcement that Richmond must be abandoned. (This was the note handed to Davis as the President attended morning services at St. Paul's Episcopal Church.) Taylor remembered Lee during this period as being "self-contained and serene." He "acted as one who was conscious of having accomplished all that was possible in the line of duty, and who was undisturbed by the adverse conditions in which he found himself." *General Lee,* p. 275.

Page 150. In his first narrative Taylor made no mention of the unusual events surrounding his marriage to Elizabeth Seldon Saunders, the daughter of a former U. S. Navy commander. The story is one of the last dashing episodes of the Confederacy. In the feverish activity of April 2, Taylor took time out to telegraph his brother, Maj. Robinson Taylor, who was serving on Gen. William Mahone's staff near Richmond, that he wished to be married that night in the capital. Robinson accordingly made the necessary arrangements. Near sundown, when all paperwork relative to the retreat had been completed, Taylor asked Lee's permission to say goodbye to his mother and sister in Richmond and to wed Miss Saunders. Lee, at first hesitant to grant so unusual a request, soon acquiesced. Taylor promptly hopped aboard a locomotive and arrived in Richmond at the height of the chaos commensurate with the evacuation of the city. Rev. Mr. Charles Minnegerode, famed rector of St. Paul's, performed the marriage ceremony in the presence of both families. "As will be readily understood," Taylor wrote later, "the occasion was not one of great hilarity, though I was very happy; my eyes were the only dry ones in the company." Near 4 A.M. the following morning, with Richmond in flames, Taylor kissed his new wife goodbye and galloped across Mayo's Bridge to rejoin Lee. See Taylor, *General Lee*, pp. 276–78; *Confederate Veteran*, XXIV (1916), 234; Sally Brock Putnam, *In Richmond during the War* (New York, 1867), p. 364; Henry Kyd Douglas, *I Rode with Stonewall* (Chapel Hill, 1940), p. 330.

Page 151. Owing to frequent raids by Federal cavalry on the slowly moving Confederate wagon train, Taylor placed all headquarters records in a small chest and ordered the guards to destroy them should the danger arise of their falling into Federal hands. On April 6 a Federal force struck the train near the headquarters wagon; nervous guards immediately burned the chest and its contents. "As events proved," Taylor lamented after the war, this action was "a precaution quite unnecessary and occasioning irreparable loss." *General Lee,* pp. 280–81.

Page 153. Taylor omitted the first exchange of words between Lee and Meade. The Confederate commander was riding back to his headquarters when a small group of bluecoated horsemen intercepted him. "Good morning, General," a large, bearded, hawknosed officer said cheerfully. Lee peered at the man thoughtfully, trying to identify the faintly familiar features. Suddenly he realized that this was George G. Meade, commander of the Army of the Potomac and a close friend in days gone by. After an exchange of warm greetings, Lee asked: "But what are you doing with all that gray in your beard?" Meade, in magnanimous style, promptly replied: "You have to answer for most of it !" Theodore Lyman, *Meade's Headquarters, 1863–65,* edited by G. R. Agassiz (Boston, 1922), p. 360.

Page 154. Taylor erred in stating that Lee arrived in Richmond

on April 12. Lee did not leave Appomattox until late in the afternoon of that date. Taylor corrected this slip subsequently in his
General Lee, p. 296.

Page 160. The effective strength of the Army of Northern Virginia on April 1, 1865, was closer to 33,000 men. Taylor's figure
of 43,500 probably included all Confederate troops in Virginia as
well as those under Wade Hampton, who had been dispatched to
confront Sherman's army in North Carolina.

INDEX.

JAMES I. ROBERTSON, JR. is Alumni Distinguished Professor of History at Virginia Tech. A noted Civil War historian, Professor Robertson served as Executive Director of the Civil War Centennial Commission.